# LOVE & TAXES

## Book 1.

### Written By

## Erica S. Elliott

ARNICA PRESS

Published by ARNICA PRESS

www.ArnicaPress.com

Cover Art by Erica S. Elliott

www.EricaSwensonElliott.com

Printed in the United States of America.

ISBN: 978-1-7336446-0-0

This work is a memoir. It reflects the author's present recollections of her experiences over a period of years. Certain names, locations, and identifying characteristics have been changed, and certain individuals are composites. Dialogue and events have been recreated from memory and, in some cases, have been compressed to convey the substance of what was said or what occurred. This book is also designed to provide information, education and motivation to our readers. The author and publisher are not offering it as legal, accounting, or other professional services advice. The author and publisher make no representations or warranties of any kind and assume no liabilities of any kind with respect to the accuracy or completeness of the contents and specifically disclaim any implied warranties of merchantability or fitness of use for a particular purpose. Neither the author nor the publisher shall be held liable or responsible to any person or entity  with respect to any loss or financial, commercial, incidental or consequential   damages caused, or alleged to have been caused, directly or indirectly, by the information contained herein. Every company is different and the advice and  strategies contained herein may not be suitable for your situation. If legal advice        is required, the services of a competent professional person should be sought.

# Book 1.

# How it all began

A true Story

# Erica S. Elliott

ARNICA PRESS

LOVE & TAXES  by Erica S. Elliott

# TABLE OF CONTENTS

*Sweet Keith,*

*One day you told me,*

*"You were such an adventurous soul, but you hadn't had any real adventures. I wanted to make it my mission to change that."*

*Well, I must say, you have achieved your objective!*

# WHERE TO BEGIN

Things are not always as they appear. Keith's Story, my story, then our story, where to start? It began a long time ago, but that depends on perspective doesn't it? The ride has been fast and furious, so it often feels like a few fleeting moments. It all began on that first night we met, but one could argue even before. That evening, we sat for hours, as Keith wove stories from his life. Such huge events of magnificent grandeur comparative to my more modest life of reading, studying, observing, listening to people, and applying the rules of taxation to clients' facts and circumstances.

I believe, our mutual storytelling is a cornerstone of Keith and Me. Over the years, as I listened to Keith share his pithy wisdom wrapped in practical advice, I knew they belonged in print. So, I started to write this book simply as a method to capture Keith's valuable business advice to preserve and share with others. Then it morphed of its own accord into something deeper.

There is that infamous generation born in between the two of us, the Baby Boomers. Keith is a few years ahead of them in what some call The Silent

Generation as referenced in a 1951 Time Magazine article. In 2008, one author named them in the title of his book *The Lucky Few*. As one can imagine, there weren't as many children born during World War II. All the parents were off to war or factories in supportive roles. When Keith's generation grew up, they were busy birthing industries and careers that are givens in our age today.

And I am a few years behind the Baby Boomers in Generation X. We were the lucky few born despite the birth control pill, newly dispensed. We had our own levels of paranoia shaped by stark messages of death by nuclear fallout from the interminable cold war. And if we were one of the chosen few to survive radiation poisoning, we would surely die from the mysterious terrifying scourge of AIDS. We were quaintly categorized in the memorable movie, *The Breakfast Club*, where we all fit into one particular stereotype or another as seen through the lens of the Baby Boomers.

Therefore, as Keith lived his business career before mine, he had so much valuable experience. When we came together, Keith naturally shared his wisdom with me often told in memorable stories. Each story could be entertaining or eye opening, but each held at least one nugget of wisdom. Today as an entrepreneur, I have applied many of his principles to my own decisions. I've also observed many of my peers take Keith's thoughtful advice and instill it  their own lives.

Besides being interesting globe-trotting business stories, they also contain mutable formulas for success, as one of our friends pointed out.  They are timeless principles that worked in previous decades, but can be modified and applied in today's techno-world.

As our industrial world is dismantled one brick at a time, the hierarchy and corporate structure that was available to Keith's generation through mine as a training ground, aren't as readily available.  Yes, we have a proliferation of search engines that can mine the ever-expanding universe of content. The ability to directly access knowledge without having to receive permission from gate keepers is now unprecedented. Well, at least the physical ones, we haven't identified all the virtual Keepers yet have we?

But yet, something has been lost.  The business world continues to be re-shaped. There are fewer institutions with less layers of mid-level jobs as technological automations replace them.  Naturally, this is fueling the explosion of entrepreneurial endeavors in this country.  One can argue from necessity.  But as every entrepreneur knows, when you start your own business, there is no experienced manager down the hall to help you figure out a problem in one minute.  You are on your own.  Yes, you can ask Google or Alexa, but only if you know what the question is to ask. And the one thing that the web doesn't do so well is hold a candle while you fumble in the dark trying to build the next new gadget in your basement.

I've spent the last few years partnering with young entrepreneurs of the next generation. We work in new ways, over web-based conference calls, sitting on the cloud stationed around the world, which is superbly efficient. Yet, countless times I have heard, "I wish someone had taught me this in school! Why don't we ever learn something practical like this? If there was only someone that had told me!" They glean as much knowledge from Ted Talks and training videos that they can, but there is an overarching framework missing, a cry for a "gray haired" mentor. Accidentally, I have come to realize that the gray-haired mentor is now me!

So besides being a love story, this book is for the fearless entrepreneurs out there, blazing a solitary new path. I hope that our combined business stories forged in the last fires of the industrial age will light your way. For there is underlying mutable formulae for creative success that transcends time. There is a myriad of solutions to problems, but they descend from a few tried and true principles. From our view, these principles all derive from one overarching principle, the Golden Rule. This has not changed. Do unto others as you would have them do unto you, then magical things can happen.

One may call, Keith's valuable advice, salty or downright in-your-face direct, but nevertheless words of wisdom. Keith was raised in South Carolina. Even though he lost a lot of his southern accent working in Yankee country, he utilizes many of the South's colloquial expressions when he talks. In my view, this verbal technique of advice wrapped in stories makes his wisdom more memorable. Upon reflection, I knew how much they changed me and others for the better, partly because one can more easily recall the story. It became important to me to write it all down, as best as I could, before time passes us by and the opportunity is gone.

But as these business stories came to life with each keystroke, it became clear that there was another story waiting to be told. At times it was quite demanding about it too. It is our love story.

Over the years, people were often curious about how the two of us had come together from different social sets, geographies and generations. Often strangers could be quite rude about their assumptions. But we attempted to remind ourselves that this nastiness was often borne from their own personal suffering, readily readable on their scowling faces. When some would ask how we came to be a couple, often I would joke that it was definitely Love and Taxes.

Since this is actually true, it became apparent about half way through the writing of this book, that it was also the perfect title. For this book is based on both the true events of our business lives and our love story.

In the beginning, I wasn't sure how to combine romance with business chronicles, but as more words came to the page it became simple and clear. It was just like the mixed-up hodge-podge we call life, where everything is connected and influences everything else. I include a phrase at the beginning and end of each section. Many of these are proverbs that Keith or me have coined or co-opted then repeated over the years. But they are meant as a take away from each story to be applied in your own life as you see fit. This first book focuses on our beginning, that night where we stood at an intersection with hurricane force winds of change at our backs.

I hope our story will light the way as you wend through this maze of business adventures that I have gathered here for you. And yes, truth is often wilder than fiction.

*~ Be open to the Unexpected ~*

# HAUNTINGLY FAMILIAR

*~ Facts matter so use your own Judgment ~*

It was a weird feeling to be so at home with a stranger I had never met before, well at least in this lifetime. Reminiscent of old home week, everything was "hauntingly familiar", to quote Stevie Knicks. Suddenly, I heard the "Voice Over the Phone", this retired Chairman and CEO of a publicly traded multi-national corporation. His tough but fair reputation had far preceded him in our existing phone relationship. Partners in my huge accounting firm, warned me how formidable Keith could be. This was coming from men pretty intimidating themselves. One even said, that I better be on guard, because they had never been spoken to "in that way before".

But let me go back and begin before I met The Voice that fateful night. There were already many little signs beforehand that intrigued me about him. Over my career, there were a number of clients whom referenced this same man, R. Keith Elliott. Each registered a level of awe-struck wonder over Keith's rain making capabilities and how he made "sh*t happen". Over the years of our phone relationship, I would wonder about the actual man behind The Voice,

15

because I wanted to reconcile these conflicting perceptions for myself. This was back when the internet was beginning and you couldn't google someone's name and get images from the last five years of their life. People remained a voice over the phone, quite often for forever. But this was not going to be one of those times.

So that first fateful night, when we sat catty corner for dinner, unbeknownst to ourselves, we began the fascinating puzzle of the most complex and rewarding relationship of our lives. For me I was captured by Keith's stories of life, business, global travel. They weren't just random stories of fluff; they were parabolic in an Aesop's Fables kind of way. They had meaning, purpose and his principles were so timelessly on point in various life applications.

When still a child, but already an obsessive observer of people, one of my first determinative rules of social engagement was that two adults' versions of an interaction never matched. Sometimes I could barely recognize the facts. I knew the grown-ups weren't lying to me. They both emphatically believed their version of events was the only truth. And that is how I forged one of my first principles about people: Perception Shapes Reality. In today's world of 2019, this is quite commonly understood, but back in my 1970's childhood, not so much. In these pages you will read my observational memoir, which is based on how my brain has chosen to forge my own

Perception of Reality. Other participants in this story may not agree with the events I lay out here, but that is the beauty of a memoir, they don't have to. They can go and write their own book, because this story is my own.

*~ Perception shapes Reality ~*

# BUT YOU DON'T LOOK LIKE
# A TAX ACCOUNTANT

*~ Always be True to yourself*
*regardless of Others ~*

By the time I met Keith, my fifteen-year career was one hundred percent focused on working with very wealthy and powerful people, helping them with their personal financial services.  I loved going on the road and meeting them in their natural habitat, instead of the antiseptic, impersonal office.  Just like any group of people, some were great, or happy, some miserable and others awful.  I tended to categorize my clients into three groups:  Inherited Wealth, Corporate Executives and Entrepreneurs.  After meeting lots of people in each of these groups, they were quite distinctive in their character traits.  After some time, I became pretty adept at predicting each people group's responses to my questions and recommendations for their consideration.  More on these personality types later.

This first half of my thirty-year career was spent inside the machine of two Big Four Public Accounting Firms. When I started work, they were known as the Big Eight.  My endearing nickname for my own employer was the Matrix, you know like Keanu Reeves wandering around in the ether of a parallel universe.

The rapid reduction in the number of competitors, from Eight to Four happened over a decade spanning the nineties and early two-thousands. I christened the survivors the Final Four. I say Final because the government secretly regretted its decision to ignore Paul Volcker's admonition to resist the regulatory censure of Arthur Andersen, which caused its rapid demise. The regulatory powers aren't going to let the Big Four dwindle to the Final Few, because there will be even less competitive pricing in the world of gargantuan audits on T-Rex sized global corporations. Arthur Andersen, some would argue the mightiest of the Eight, others would say the most arrogant, is now gone forever from the face of the earth. Poof, up in smoke, along-side and because of Enron's evaporation. As the accounting firm was tarred and feathered as a partnership, partners offering pearls of knowledge were tarnished as well. So, they just picked up their remaining marbles and went across the street to the other few firms. Like many other industrial roll ups, today the cost of excruciating regulatory transparency has quadrupled the fees charged for an audit of a publicly held corporation.

But back to our objection, if you look at my photograph on the back cover of this book, and read my casual, prosy writing style, none of this fits YOUR stereotype of an accountant. We all know the jokes, the green eyeshades and pocket protectors, comments such as "only an accountant would understand this gobbledygook".

So, you probably have the unspoken objection in your mind that I had to answer many times throughout the course of my career: "But you don't look like a tax accountant!" Funny right? We humans can't help ourselves, we are quite presumptive in how things should look.

So how did I get here and break all of the standard physical requirements of the euphemistic accountant that exists in your brain? Well that is a good question. Initially, I would say fear. It was the eternal human quest for personal autonomy, if one uses the politically correct term, otherwise known as the outright fear for survival. So, it goes to prove that humans can do just about anything to survive, even taxes. And then there is some magical moment along the way where surviving becomes thriving.

My eventual evolution into thriving, I think has something to do with my really cool yet unusual upbringing. My Dad was a community organizer before politicians coopted the term. He was the Reverend Jon E. Swenson, and his calling was to help others, whom he passionately loved. But everyone called him by his nickname, The Rev, an endearing tweak on his title. Often, he would joke his memoir would be titled *The Steeple and the Street*. He was kind of a Jesus Movement pastor for the people. This group was a break out subset of the Hippies that evolved during the seventies. When these flower children woke up from their Purple Haze, they came to church (well, some churches that let them in) where Jesus helped them get clean. And my Pop's church was one of them. Pop wanted to help people find a better way for themselves. This was an awesome way to be raised, but it was also terrifying. For it was all about trust and that the Lord would provide for all of our needs through dependence on church going members, some quite dictatorial and others downright unstable.

We lived in a parsonage, which is a house owned by the church for a minister and family. Pop was paid once a month, and by the last week of every month, there was no more money to go food shopping until the first of the month rolled around again. What was in the house is what we had to eat. There was always enough, but not necessarily anything one would choose. Tissue boxes were too expensive, so toilet paper served a dual purpose as tissues too. Ordering a pizza was a big deal, it was a luxury. You get the point.

Obviously, this upbringing isn't one of a kind, and many children are food deprived today. But I would argue we all have a choice. The one thing each of us has is a very big brain. And the cool thing about this free country, is we are still allowed to use it. I was going to use the only asset I had, my brain. No matter what, I was going to college so I could get a job in business. I had no idea what that meant, because I

didn't know too many business people. I knew a lot
of teachers, academics, church and blue-collar people.
But I was going to earn my own way. I was tired of
not being able to turn on the air conditioner, because
the church trustee paying the electric bill was going to
complain about it.


*~ Find your own Way for it is*
*the most Meaningful ~*

# MY FIRST CLIENT CONSULT AND THE FIFTY-FIFTY METHOD

*~ Listen to others to understand their Fears ~*

But often unknown to ourselves, we are quite born to do certain things. And I was definitely born as a financial advisor, I just wasn't aware of it yet. My first accidental financial planning consultation happened when I was twelve years old.

It was about 1981 and my Dad was given an option in his minister's defined benefit pension plan, to make a special election. He had a one-time chance to opt in to create an additional personal pre-tax contribution to his retirement fund from his modest paycheck.

My Dad could care less about this kind of stuff, so he passed the buck to my Mom. My Mom was really good with numbers but she was downright terrified of making the wrong choice. She could clearly see that she would be taking away precious current dollars from our family's small monthly cash flow to fund a future retirement benefit. And what if she selected the wrong investments, and the future

benefit was diminutive?  In her mind, it was a Sophie's
Choice kind of moment.  It would all be her fault, her
children "starving to death" presently or she and Pop
would be an undue burden on her children in old age.

This timeframe was the beginning of the death
of future defined benefit plans, where companies were
responsible to fund retired employees.  As a child at
that time, I had no clue. People were starting to live
longer, companies started to break up faster,
shareholders clamored for greater profits, and life-long
careers at one company came to a screeching halt.
These company benefits were being offloaded onto
individuals for self-funding.  No one knew what the
heck they were doing.  Today people are familiar with
terms such as saving for retirement and IRAs, but this
was new uncharted territory in 1981.  There were no
financial advisors for the little people.  One day they
walked out to their mailbox, pulled out the letter
opener and were apprised that they had seven days to
decide their future retirement funding.  They were
expected to brush up on exotic tax law language about
pre-tax and after-tax elections and investment options.
Battalions of lawyers wrote in micro print about the
retirement world upended, as if you were an idiot if
you questioned this golden opportunity to enrich
yourself.

Of course, being the present-day entrepreneur
that I am, I must point out that defined benefit plans
somehow do live on quite healthily in the public sector

of government jobs. The regulators who tell the rest of us what to do, are all buttoned up with lifelong benefits. Important but lower paying jobs such as teachers, firemen and policeman come with some sort of pension. How do you think people stay (often unhappily) in these secure but lower paying jobs? It's the play on fear, the hook of the safety net of the pie-in-the-sky future guaranteed retirement benefit. Unless of course, people in charge of the pension fund abscond with it, such as the Teamsters Union did with the Drake's Cakes fund, but that is a story for my next book.

That particular day, I met with my Mother in my Dad's study where he wrote his sermons surrounded by his beloved books. You remember the seventies press board wood paneling? Well it lined the walls in the walk-out basement of our split-level parsonage. Besides the damp faint scent of mildewed books, I could smell my Mother's fear. For an hour or two, we read aloud abstract technical terms about qualified pension money. The more we read, the less sure Mom was. She was slowly becoming debilitated by fear, the deer in headlights effect.

It was a pivotal moment for me in my budding career of financial advisor. At that point I knew that ANY decision was better than none. If we did nothing, he would have no future opportunity to elect into this special deferral. We had to do something. So, I came up with my Fifty-Fifty Method that later as an adult I used many times, when clients were stymied with indecision.

Mom and I opted in and got the clock running. Then we selected a middle of the road deferral amount, not the maximum, not the minimum. Then we picked a conservative investment choice for the deferred dollars. At least we picked something. Then we backed into the impact on their net monthly cash flow and revised a budget. By the end of our session my Mother was laughing with relief. It was an important lesson for me: Fear Kills. It is better to keep moving, don't freeze.

The second big lesson I learned that day, I now term: The Fifty-Fifty Method. If you aren't confident in a future outcome, don't go all in, do half. For example, not sure if you should buy a stock? Only use half of your budget, and buy fifty percent of what you could buy. Not sure if you should sell? Sell half to ensure you don't lose it all. Yes, it is simple advice, but it surprises me how often humans think only in black and white: "Am I all in or all out?" Try straddling the fence sometimes. It is a way to get your feet wet, test the waters and yet not drown.

Thirty years later, this one pivotal investment decision was the difference maker in my parents' ability to buy their first and only home upon retirement. It was their down payment.

So, whatever it is that is natural to you to do, don't listen to other people, just do it. To this day, it is one of the most satisfying feelings for me to help alleviate fear and consternation in others' lives. Bringing order out of financial chaos. So yes, I am a tax accountant.

*~ Your Destiny will choose You ~*

# HOW DID I GET HERE?

### ~ *Know Thyself* ~

Once I graduated from my comfy cozy little Christian Liberal Arts college on the Main Line of Philadelphia, I needed a job. I had a B.S. in Business Administration. After listening to one of my professor's rattle on about how difficult the CPA exam was to pass, I fearfully avoided the Accounting degree. Ironically, this cowardly decision led me to receive a job offer from the number one public accounting firm in the world at that time, Arthur Andersen. They had a job posting for a new position in the Tax Department, someone to work a new-fangled computer to prepare personal tax returns. In 1989, desktop computers were scarce and brand new.

I recall, all the agita of that first interview. Having to borrow a car to drive down the Schuylkill Expressway into center city Philadelphia. Schuylkill is pronounced School-kill. Some historians believe it comes from the Dutch word for skulk or hide. But the area was historically resident to the Lenape. Many of their tribal names adhere to local places still such as Manayunk, Wissahickon and Conshohocken. Therefore, there is an argument that Schuylkill is a native word for hidden creek. Since this named expressway was carved out of the side of the mountain, it had all kinds of meandering dangerous curves for a boatload of daily commuter traffic. As locals we nicknamed it the "Sure-Kill", because there was usually a least one accident a day on the thing, and more often than not it seemed to be someone was dead.

On the day of my interview, I didn't have enough cash to park in any of the parking garages nearby. And I was concerned if I parked blocks away where it was free, I would be too sweaty and disheveled walking back. After estimating the time remaining before my interview, I was also concerned a hike in heels would cut way too close. As I approached the intersection at 17th and Market Streets, I spied an illegal parking space in front of a fire hydrant that was catty-corner from the building. I sent up a small prayer for protection and no fires, and parked.

I had maxed out my Strawbridge & Clothier's department store credit card to get my first wool Evan Picone interview suit. I loved it so much. It was black, with pin prick polka dots. The jacket had the awesome biggish shoulder pads of the eighties, but with a short waist, like Adam Ant used to wear in his music videos, and this feminine little ruffle around the waist. The skirt was the long pencil-type just below the knee. My head hunter Tina coached me on some important tips. Upon her advice, I figured out how to install a tight French braid bun of my long hair, so it wouldn't be a distraction. I wore three-inch heels, which put me around six feet, one inch. I felt like that would even the playing field a bit, since I could look a man of average height in the eye. I hadn't yet learned how to do a proper handshake, without getting my hand broken, but that would come later.

As the secretary led me down the hallway to the corner office, I made sure to make eye contact and smile when someone was approaching. Later, I found out how important this trait was. One of my future closest allies and business friends, Curt, was walking towards me at that moment. Much later, Curt told me what an impact that moment had on him. Everyone on the floor knew it was interview day. The fact that I was initiating friendly contact before I had a job apparently isn't that normal. And it wasn't just perfunctory, Curt later confessed, he could feel my genuine emotion.

This exchange became a symbol to me of how tiny gestures can make a future pivotal impact. As allies, Curt and I solved a lot of problems together, that perhaps would have otherwise never come to pass, if I hadn't smiled.

When I reached the corner office, it was a green light! It felt pretty natural. When I got the call with my start date, I was raring to conquer the world!

*~ No matter what, be Real ~*

# TRAINING OVERLOAD

### ~ *Learn Everything you can from Everyone* ~

I was told not to worry, they would train me in everything I needed to know. That is one thing that the firm knew how to do, train. In the first year, I probably had five hundred hours of training, which is twenty-five percent of a two thousand hour, full time year of work. We even had our world headquarters of training based in St. Charles, Illinois, at sleepy ex-burb of Chicago. I spent a few weeks there every year learning Uncle Arthur's ways.

My co-workers were Accounting majors from more prestigious schools than me, such as the University of Pennsylvania or Villanova. They were all on the traditional accounting career tracking towards partner. Since my job description was new based on this new-fangled computer, my role was considered one step down professionally. Coincidentally, two alumnae from my little college were already safely ensconced in the Tax department. Their current career successes helped vouch for my mental capacity to keep up, even though I wasn't from the "right" school.

Again, it was as if the winds of fate were at my back, blowing me into my destiny as a financial advisor. I had pictured working at an advertising firm making cool fashionista magazine ads, or being a fashion buyer for a department store, or even a clothing designer! Never once did I see myself as an accountant. I read about how fuddy-duddy they were required to dress. I LOVED fashion and I wanted to wear what I wanted to wear to work! But the opportunity to start at such a prestigious firm with a relatively secure paycheck, as long as I didn't screw up, was too enticing. I was taking the opportunity at hand.

So, out of the box, with the wrong degree from the wrong school, I was employed by the number one accounting firm in the world, because of the computer's game changing technology. Little did I know how this accidental path was really embedded in my stars. I had found my destiny, or really my destiny had found me.

One of the scariest things about learning, is the more you learn the more you realize how little you know. So, in sheer terror, I sat down at my first computer in 1989 and dug my fingernails into the desk. In college, we were required to take a one credit computer literacy course without any computers. We basically memorized terms such as bits and bytes. I touched a computer once in a brand-new lab, after signing up for "main frame access time". And I knew nothing about taxes. But the one thing I knew how to do was outwork everybody else. They were going to have to drag my body out. I knew I could be the last man standing, so to speak, every time. At least my epitaph would read, "She tried really hard." I had a career path and a pay check, I had achieved my first goal.

*~ If you give your All,*
*you will find yourself on the Journey ~*

# LEARNING AS YOU GO

### ~ *Be Kind to yourself, your mental*
### *sponge needs time to Absorb and Embed* ~

Right out of the box, I started with over one hundred hours of training. Two days of firm orientation. My first day of work was January ninth, 1989 on a blustery winter day in center city Philadelphia. While we were sitting in the corporate training room on the twenty-first floor, the heating system broke. The heater was stuck in the ON setting. Even though it was freezing outside, we were tracking North towards ninety degrees Fahrenheit. Finally, the corporate trainer said, "It is truly ok to take off your jackets, while we wait for a repairman to come." About half of us refused to cave in and remained in full uniform. I actually half-believed that it was some weird kind of hazing ritual to see who in the room would break first, and it was NOT going to be me! I would stand by my motto, and go down with the ship.

The following week, I sat through my first forty hours of taxation training so I could prepare personal income tax returns. It was the first few hours of thousands to come, but they were the most terrifying. I had never been a linguist, other languages were very difficult for me to learn. Immediately, I realized that Taxation was its own secret language. Different lecturers appeared about every two hours, happily chirping away, sharing all of their specialized knowledge.

It was definitely going to be a death by drowning in a deluge. My learning style is definitely via reading. In college, I finally learned that the only way I could retain an oral lecture, was if I took notes the entire time. Once I lifted the pen from page, my mind flitted out the window and was thinking on an entirely different plane.

Today, there are studies about how the act of doodling actually increases the brain's retention of lecture. I always found that I could digest material so much faster when reading, as I drank in the printed page. Needless to say, my eyes were riveted on my four-inch, three ring binder the entire week. My favorite Bic pen (the most reliable pen ever, so much so that they stopped making this version, since they were denigrating their own market place) locked in my fisted left hand. Scribbling down every word tumbling forth in my own illegible scrawl that only I could decipher. Over the years I often thought I could be a spy, because no one could comprehend my secret written short hand.

I slept all weekend to allow my brain to recover from its first dose of tax shock and an attempt to absorb some of it. The next week's forty hours were spent in computer training. This somehow felt easier to me, I learned how to use the firm's proprietary software as a support tool. The software could help guide me through the abstract tax forest. I likened myself to a lumberjack who was given an ax instead of a pocketknife to do my job. It was somehow more comforting, and I no longer felt so alone. I also had twenty-four hours of self-study that I was required to complete, they included a few case studies.

This technology week was led by Karen, my first direct supervisor. Karen was one of the funniest women I've ever met. She would raise her eyes to the sky, place her hands in a praying position and ask, "Dear God, can you give me a tape worm for just six weeks? I need to lose ten pounds. That's all I ask. I promise I will never bother you again. Amen!"

It was the kind of humor that was needed to break the natural tension of tax deadlines, intimidating partners and powerful clients.

*~ Find the humor in things, yes even Taxes ~*

# SEND IN THE EXPERT

### ~ *Celebrate your own Efforts in technical Expertise* ~

After finishing my first tax season, I was grateful that I was still employed. When I got my envelope of handwritten evaluations from the ten or so reviewers and managers that I prepared tax returns for, my hands were shaking. I literally ran into a bathroom stall, so I could read them in total privacy, in case I broke out in tears. Somewhat shocked, I found that I had many perfect scores and generous comments giving me A's for effort. In relief, I started crying anyway, because at least I wasn't going to get fired out of the gate!

After April fifteenth was over, I was asked to study up on the firm's proprietary fixed assets software to track depreciation for companies. I say proprietary, because my firm had to write all of its own software. There was no TurboTax or software equivalents. There was no cloud or even internet. Desktop personal computers were fairly new things and the laptop had not yet been invented.

Our software development headquarters was in Sarasota, Florida. A bunch of computer programmers built our firm's suite of custom tax software on site. Floppy 5 ¼ inch disks and then hard 3 ½ disks were programmed with the software and shipped to our own or clients' offices upon purchase for installation one desktop computer at a time.

One beautiful May morning, Mary called me down to her manager's office. I liked working for her, she took time to explain each return's issues before I started it, an efficient way to work. Mary's eyes were dancing with excitement, as she said, "We sold an important project to one of our corporate clients, they bought our Fixed Asset software and they need help implementing it. You will have to go out to the client site. It could be a couple months engagement. First you will have to install the software, then upload their inventory of fixed assets into the software to calculate depreciation for book, regular tax and AMT tax. We told them we were sending in the expert, so it will be a smooth transition. Do you think you can drive out next week?"

I couldn't help blurting out, "WHAT???" My light Philly accent probably reared its head and it sounded more like, "WHUH??? But I'm not an expert! I just started learning this stuff!"

Still with a big smile Mary reminded me, "You did just great during 1040 season. You have all that computer training. Remember, you know more than everyone else surrounding you when it comes to this new software, so you ARE the expert. And you have unlimited direct phone support, a hot line to Sarasota."

I was glad for the vote of confidence. But I could picture the myriad of bumps in the road that could happen while trying to upload 20,000 individual assets sitting alone in a client's conference room. I pictured a big red bat-phone perpetually on speaker box, as I read off endless error messages from the black background computer screen, before Windows turned all screens white. At least I got to save a little bit on not paying Philly Wage Tax while I worked outside the city, a small comfort.

That was my first on site client assignment. Immediately, I loved every minute of it. Even the technical problems were invigorating when I found resolutions on my own. Over the course of my client visitation, different employees would wander into my conference corner to talk. The client supervisor surreptitiously offered me a job, clearly not wanting my employer to know he was attempting to poach. Briefly, I imagined doing the same thing at the same place all day long, and I knew that life was not for me. I loved the jumping around to different locations and projects, I needed the exhilaration of variety and deadlines.

Sometimes it even felt like a confessional. One woman, with tears welling in her eyes, shared the horrific story of her rape by an unknown man, as he had bagged her head. In her own driveway, after work, as she bent down to get her briefcase out of the backseat, he attacked her from behind. This broke my heart. To this day, I never get in my car without glancing under the car and in the back seat.

The day I was told the rape story, my skin pricked all over me. I knew this wasn't normal behavior from clients. My peers didn't go out to clients and get job offers and victim confessions on a daily basis. Besides my hard-core work ethic, I began to see that my connection through relationships was my differentiating strength among my tax peers. Many of them were the more traditional Code Heads, whom had difficulty stringing together a conversation with other humans. They could repeat verbatim paragraphs lifted directly from the Internal Revenue Code, but not succeed in a two-way conversation.

Pretty soon, partners and managers were sending me all over Southeastern Pennsylvania to install tax software. Clients asked for me, and I loved it. Daily, I embraced the ever-changing kaleidoscope of people whom felt safe to share the stories of their lives with me while we solved their business problems together.

*~ Recognize what makes you Special ~*

# KNOW YOUR AUDIENCE

*~ Don't try to sell a hammer to a Sailor ~*

Over time, I got to work with all kinds of people as the traveling tax troubadour. I began to stereotype and categorize people. Like we all do. I came up with three client-type buckets, and most of my clients fell into one of them.

Inherited Wealth was the first type. To generalize, people born into wealth were often quite understated in their dress, even stodgy. They could literally look down their nose at me, which up until that point in my provincial life, I didn't realize was actually physically possible. They viewed their financial service providers, like myself, equivalent to their "Help". They were often terrible payers, wanted everything for free because of their superior status in life, and generally didn't want the Help to get too familiar. As the people person that I am, this annoyed me to no end, because it wasn't as easy for me to advocate when my client resisted emotional engagement. There were of course exceptions. Two of my favorite people ever, were born into wealthy families in Europe before World War II. Both of their families fled the fascist-socialist regime of Mussolini, when they as children were banned from attending elementary school due to their Jewish heritage. When I met them, they were living a healthy retired octogenarian life. The husband still published as a working academic. Culture just oozed from their pores. It was wonderful to listen to them talk about everyday life.

I remember another elderly lady who had lived her entire life on the Main Line in Philadelphia. She wrung her bejeweled, manicured hands, sitting in her beautiful breakfast room saying, "Please don't let the IRS put me in jail!" and she meant it. I wondered how it must have felt to live in quiet terror in a sunny room overlooking the manor, with the grandfather clock ticking away the minutes of one's lifetime.

Entrepreneurs were the second group of clients. In many ways they were the anti-thesis of the Inherited Wealth crowd. Most of these guys founded a privately held family business, or continued to operate an entity as a generational successor. This realm included a lot of real estate professionals and retail or light industrial owner/operators. These Entrepreneurs wore their arrogance in a different way. They were brash and bold as opposed to refined and snippy. Their business was the first love of their lives, it was their baby. Often their wives and children ran a distant second and third to the business they built from an idea into a money-making empire. Some of my most successful clients in this arena utilized a tandem team approach, the proverbial front man and back house man.

The front man was the Sales personality, that could sell anything to anyone. The back-house man, was typically the numbers guy, who made the operation run like a fine-tuned machine. They had figured out years before how to meld their polar strengths into complimentary pieces. These Entrepreneurs were a lot of fun. But trying to collect tax information from the Front Man was nigh on impossible. One year, I remember getting the final tax receipt from the wife on the last possible day. It had a gigantic footprint on the envelope where it had resided in the man's car for the previous four months. Often, they were very AD&D before that was an identifiable term, and consequently everyone loved them.

The third bucket my clients fell into was the corporate executives. I prepared taxes for a bunch of well-heeled lawyers, bankers, CEOs, CFOs, Treasurers all from publicly traded companies and subsequently retired executives. This group was hard pressed due to their own careers' requirements. Time was of the essence with them. Well most of them. The bankers seemed to have all the time in the world, as I saw it. They were always gone by five thirty, had all of these extra holidays and would be bragging about their golf handicaps. Golf? Who had time for golf? It was a slow day if I made time for lunch.

As a whole, these executives were very organized compared to the other two categories. They were much more impressive with numbers than I could ever achieve. Blistering shows of mental math, calculating rates of return in their heads as if it was kindergarten. I would madly try to memorize every page of their tax return before meeting with them, so I'd be as prepared as possible.

A few of them were sneaky, which I could read in their eyes. There would be this brief point in their glance, where they had the hypnotic gaze of a snake, charming its prey, right before it strikes. When I saw this look, I knew there was some trap being laid, some important fact being withheld, some artificial deductions being shuffled into the pile, some tax liability they were trying to offload from their balance sheet onto me and my firm. And that wasn't going to happen.

A few of them wore bespoke beautiful suits made in London just for them. Walking into their executive C-Suites, I imagined was similar to entering the halls of royal courts of old. You hope to not just survive, but prove your worth and relevancy so one is not exiled to the dungeons. This group was the most daunting for me to deal with, because of their own statistical wielding prowess and corporate power. Yet often, when I had penetrated the fortress, this group could be the most rewarding for me. I could learn so much that was applicable in my own career.

Little did I know how true this would be about Keith. He was one of these retired CEOs. He was a battle-scarred corporate warrior with many wise, war stories secreted away in his soul. Each person has a book inside of them. If you can learn to read it you will find some wisdom that is important for you to embed and spread. There are no accidents, each person is in your life for a reason. As time went by, it became clear to me, that there were also reasons I was in Keith's life. One, was as a preservationist of history, a sort of secrets keeper. The archivist's role is to protect knowledge, yet also share it when the time is right. Embedded here are the stories of Keith.

*~ Everyone has a Story Book inside of Them ~*

# FOX HOLE COMPANIONS

*~ Trust those who Uplift and Protect You ~*

When I was back in my twenties, I could recall pretty much every conversation, the month and the location where it had occurred.  I thought everyone could do that.  Now that I'm in my fifties, I wish I still had that gift, or at least appreciated it more when I still had it.  Practicing denial, I pretend that the reason I can't find my keys and cell phone at the same time, is due to having a lot more stuff in my head now instead of natural aging.

In 1996, I remember one introductory vivid conversation that began with a CFO's personal tax preparation.  His name was Michael.  But when he began discussing Keith Elliott, one of the members of his Board of Directors, Michael started tearing up with real tears. Basically, he said that there was no one else he would rather have in a fox hole with him than Keith.  Who was this guy, Keith?  It would be seven more years before I first spoke with Keith on the phone and began to find out for myself.

As the CFO, Mike, reported to Keith and his Board of Directors, so this was highly unusual for him to have such positive strong feelings. The Board acts like the Supreme Court. They don't actually do anything. They provide strategy, act as a sounding board. They tell management what they did wrong and approve or disapprove business decisions. It can be a great relationship between management and the Board of Directors, but it can also be fraught with conflict.

Today, I vividly recall Keith's own caustic comments about having to report to a particular Board President, his old boss: "I compared him to a sexual advisor. If I wanted his f*cking advice, I would have asked for it!"

Years later, I found that Mike the CFO was probably referring to an executive incentive compensation plan that "knocked the ball out of the park", in Keith's vernacular. Keith had convinced the rest of board that if their goal was to increase shareholder value and position the entity for growth, you had to make the compensation plan commensurate with their business' goals. Once the board voted on Keith's recommendations, Mike shot the business into the next stratosphere. He was incentivized to do so, because the company's growth was now linked to his own bonus plan. But this is a deeper story that we will save and explore together later.

This level of integrity assigned to Keith wasn't all that apparent in looking at his peers. Yes, there were a number that had similar ethics. But there were also enough that clearly did not. Often, I watched executives figuratively circle each other like snarling dogs, determining how best to go for each other's throats, or even worse, mine. So, to hear one speak so highly of one of his peers, was really something.

Then a few years later, I was working on a phone call with a client. This was a widow of a young, shining executive, Reid Frazier. Reid's star burned out way too soon. She was sobbing on the phone with me about the sudden death of her husband, and how generous and supportive the CEO, Keith Elliott, had been in executing and distributing the corporate death benefits to her and her young family. The widow told me of how Keith had selected her husband as his successor to be the next CEO, which would have been a double or triple promotion if Reid had lived.

Ironically, I had just finished working for another young widow of a partner in my own accounting firm, and that widow had NOTHING good to say about my employer, its partners or our human resources department. So again, I had this information about how principled and right this man behaved when nothing was good in the world.

*~ During the worst of times,*
*a person's Truest Self is Revealed ~*

# FAIR WARNING

*~ Reserve judgment until you have More Data*
*rather than Less ~*

Another few years went by, lots of things changed, but as usual much remained the same. My firm merged with another behemoth making us the largest accounting firm in the world with one hundred and sixty-thousand employees. Walt Mahler's hilarious comparison of two dinosaurs mating to a mega-merger, makes me laugh every time because it has the virtue of being true! One, of my counterparts, Kate, left the firm after trying to juggle a career and three children. I was still trying to manage with only two children, so kudos to Kate.

I was assigned to about sixty of her clients, and one of them was the Voice Over the Phone, R. Keith Elliott. By this time, Keith had retired as CEO and Chairman of Hercules of Wilmington, Delaware. This town is a forty-five minute drive South of Philadelphia. Accountant relationships die hard, harder than Bruce Willis. Accountants are so embedded, clients will often wait until their accountant dies before finding a replacement. Keith was a raging example. Yes, he had moved to Florida, but he would rather FedEx, fax and email with the firm that knew him like the back of their hand. Even when the actual person was swapped out, they were staying with the firm that signed their tax return every year for continuity and security. It is easier to trade out bankers and lawyers than your accountant, the necessary evil so to speak.

Even though retired, Keith still worked hard on several publicly traded, companies' boards. This transition was the beginning of our phone relationship. At this time, my boss, reviewed in detail all the clients that transitioned to me and I still recall his words, "Keith Elliott was a big rainmaker. He did lots of deals, merger and acquisition type stuff. He's really tough. I want you to become the main point person on Keith's account. But the first few phone calls, I want you to sit down with me and we will review everything you will discuss beforehand. We want a seamless transition." In other words, I'm going to make sure you don't screw this up.

Then I had another surprise visitor in my office, another peer, whom had resigned from Keith's account, before Kate. This team member was really smart, had triple degrees, the CPA, passed the bar exam in numerous states and was a walking encyclopedia of fun tax facts.

"Erica, I have to give you Fair Warning about my experience with Keith Elliott! When our boss, was putting me up for partner, he sent me to meet with

Keith down at Hercules. Do you know what Keith said to me? 'What is your boss trying to do by sending me the second string?' Well, I've never been talked to that way before in my life, and I wasn't going to stand for it! I marched back to our office, and put my foot down by resigning from Keith's account," he ended in a huff.

By this point I had a small smile on my face, because I knew Keith fit into the category I coined "the warrior type". When a Warrior spoke like this it was not to be taken as a put down. This was more of friendly game of jousting, in the masculine style that men prefer. This was more of a poking the bear to see what would happen. The Warrior wants to determine if you will be able to fight with him in the trenches, are you strong enough to take the proverbial punch?

I remember laughing, and responding, "Didn't you tell him, he just got upgraded?"

*~ Consider how to convert an attack*
*into Connection ~*

# NO MORE MICKEY MEOWING

*~ Be aware when you are Poking the Bear ~*

The first time I jousted with a Warrior was my dear own Grandpop, whom was cut from this same Warrior cloth. He had a deep bass voice. He worked the shipyards for Sunoco company as an oil rigger and he smoked like a chimney. Now as a small child, I had terrible asthma, and Grandpa was the only person in my tiny universe that smoked. It was shocking to me, so much so that I nicknamed him Smokestack. I even signed his holiday cards with my signature drawing of such. At the time, I didn't understand, but Nana and my parents were much more nervous about poking the bear. Because Grandpa could be quite alarmingly vocal, if you touched the wrong nerve.

As an example, Grandpa had lost a lot of his hearing, I'm sure from working around heavy machinery his whole life, before OSHA existed and required hearing protection on the job. One family holiday, the five of us grandchildren, were upstairs playing, squealing and laughing. Suddenly, we heard Grandpa, the Bear bellowing from the bottom of the steps. As the oldest grandchild, I went to the top of the steps, to protect the little ones cowered in the hallway. Grandpa the Bear was red in the face, shaking his upraised hand in the air, bellowing "NO MORE MICKEY MEOWING!!!". This was Grandpa's favorite term for our loud play. Before I knew it, I asked the honest question, "But Grandpa you are deaf so how can you hear us?" Now Grandpa was speechless with rage over my impudent question. He didn't know what to say and spun back to the kitchen. And with that we started laughing and playing again.

That day, I learned an important principle. Be brave and speak truth to power. But there is risk, in this, of course. Throughout history many people have died because they spoke unpopular truths. We can start with Jesus Christ, Joan of Arc, Martin Luther King to name just a few. I truly didn't mean to hurt my beloved Grandpa's feelings, which I knew I inadvertently did. So that day, I began a quest of how to speak truth to others in a subtler way so they can hear the message. If you enrage someone so much with your truth telling, your advice is lost in the sea of adrenaline roaring in their ears. Today, I use humor, subtlety, imagery, parables and examples to impart advice when I work with people. These verbal tools allow the person to hear recommendations they might not like.

*~ Find your style in speaking Truth*
*so that it is Heard ~*

# THE VOICE OVER THE PHONE

### ~ *Listen to your Body as it sends signals via Emotion* ~

After being assigned to Keith's account, we began the first phase of our relationship, which was phone and email based. This is before smart phones and texting, so I should say it was landline-phone based! Everyone's business cards had multiple numbers for home line, vacation home, fax machine, a cell phone, sometimes an email address. After a few exchanges, there were still a few items required to complete Keith's personal tax return. The Executive Types, liked email, it was efficient for them. They were first adapters, because my other two client buckets often didn't even have an email address. This is before Amazon and buying stuff online. I spent a lot of time crafting emails for corporate executives, so they could quickly know what was needed and minimize time spent on their side.

Executives didn't have time for idle chit chat on the phone. Some of my Inherited Wealth Types, wanted to talk for hours, because they had time and were often quite reclusive, so they were lonely as well.

The Executive Crowd considered Time as the enemy, they never had enough of it.

These tax returns were serious deals for big time executives. Corporate officers were in the papers often for how they voted on Boards. The press loved to Monday morning quarterback their business strategy decisions and the resulting impact on their company's stock price. They were under constant scrutiny by financial analysts, the public, the press and the government. Over the years, I've heard Keith say many times, "I got my report card each and every day, when the stock exchange closed and our share price posted." How would you feel if your paycheck was covered in the business section of the local paper, in relation to your daily performance on the job? As a Big Four accounting firm service provider, we didn't want to be in the paper either, by making a stupid mistake on an executive's taxes.

I had to give Keith a call to wrap up a few missing items, to ensure tax return perfection. This time, phone call accuracy trumped email efficiency. I started working on my detailed double-spaced checklist, so I could just run down the open points quickly, and get him off the phone and back into his busy life.

We've all experienced a sense of déjà vu at some point in our lives. And this first phone call was one of them for me. Keith's voice was so resonant, not necessarily the deepest voice you've ever heard, but a rich, luxurious baritone. I remember the tiny hairs inside of my ear vibrating when he spoke. I was so rattled, I had to quickly get back down to my notes, because it was as if I was speaking to an old friend from elementary school after many years had passed. How weird! Now I understood how my peers were easily intimidated, Keith's vocal prowess alone could easily be overwhelming. I recall having a specific question about a large charitable contribution, and its validity. When asked, Keith's energy jumped up a notch as he growled, "That is a deductible item!" To which I responded with a chuckle, "When you prove it, I will deduct it." And then we laughed together.

*~ Deliver Truth firmly yet Fondly ~*

# TRAVELING THE WORLD AND CHEMISTRY

## ~ *Remember to take a Look around You* ~

Keith's business life had taken him all over the world. In his last run as CEO of Hercules, the business had over fifty-six major operating plants in over thirty countries. I recall hearing Keith say over the years, "I made it a point to visit our operating plants around the world. I was a walk around manager. I needed to see the white of their eyes, so I could tell if the operators were lying to me or not." It was a complex sprawling empire that needed constant management and every ounce of Keith's intellect and creativity to stay relevant, viable in the ever changing, competitive world of specialty chemicals. He kept a simple green plastic file folder with a laminated list of his top annual goals, which included items such as these:

1. Visit top ten global customers and suppliers

2. Visit top ten shareholders

3. Surprise visit thirty operating plants

4. Buy Something Major!

5. Incentive Pay for Bands 1, 2, 3

6. At least one new board member

Today, we have all become accustomed to the complicated products that we use on a daily basis, so much so that we are almost blind to them. We blithely talk about how we only use "natural and organic" retail items. Yet, the simple product of toilet paper is a complicated business. Yes, it is a paper product and any paper item is only created by the use of specialty chemicals. It takes huge machines, a large water supply (large defined as a river basin) and a unique set of chemicals to make toilet paper, so we literally don't have to get our hands dirty anymore wiping our own a$$.

At one point in the 1990's, Hercules supplied the majority of paper and water-treatment chemicals to the world. After decades of corporate roll ups to squeeze every penny out of stock price value for the corporate shareholders, there are only a few remaining global chemical companies. The ghost of corporate giants like Hercules haunt the hallways of reborn mega-corporations today.

*~ Keep a daily image of the Big Picture in front of You ~*

# THE REVLON DOCTRINE

### ~ *Changes in Law can have unforeseen future Impact* ~

To drill down on a major impetus of corporate roll-ups, the acceleration of corporate mergers and acquisitions can be traced back to one seminal court case that began in the 1980's, The Revlon Case. (Well at least according to the dinner table discussions at Chez Elliott.) At that time, Delaware had anointed itself as the Business-Friendly State. You didn't have to have any operations (ergo Nexus in the Tax World) in the actual state to be classified as a Delaware Company. Therefore, many large entities incorporated themselves in the state of Delaware, even though they operated in other states and countries. Therefore, the outcome of the Revlon case affected all businesses incorporated in the state of Delaware, who's ever expanding portfolio was now as proliferate as the twinkling stars of the Milky Way. Based on the many multi-national corporations choosing Delaware for tax savings and other protections that they could pass on to their shareholders, the Revlon Case was just like The Big Asteroid that hits the Atlantic Ocean and wipes out the eastern seaboard of the United States. It became rightfully known as the Revlon Doctrine.

The Chancery Court of Delaware changed the
corporate world as we know it today. The Board of
Directors of any publicly traded corporation, was now
REQUIRED to focus on the short-term interest of
the shareholders INSTEAD of what was best for the
corporate institution they represented, when they were
deciding to sell a company. That made every company
more vulnerable to hostile takeovers by corporate
raiders. It meant that you as an officer, no longer had
the right to defend the institutions' right to live, if you
were depriving the stockholders from a bigger payout.
To get down to brass tacks: WE are the stockholders
of America, even if you only have a measly IRA, a
401(k), a cushier teacher's pension at an F School or a
Stash account, YOU are part of the problem.

There are still a few remaining ways to counter
these measures. Incorporate in a state such as
Pennsylvania, where the fiduciary duty is first to the
corporation's right to all constituencies, such as
customers, vendors, employees as well as shareholders.

But probably the best way to save yourself is to
abstain from taking your private company public.
Once you are public, the happiness of your
shareholders is now more important than yours, your
customers, employees and vendors. You can keep
dancing to your own beat.

But if the cash buy out gets too provocative, I
suggest selling out to private equity or a hedge fund
with a walk away clause. That way you can be far away

on a yacht in St. Bart's, when the vultures start dissecting the carrion that was once the company that you birthed.

A current example of this travesty would be Elon Musk and his grand intentions to have the world participate in space travel.

*~Don't give away your Power, until you are ready to completely Wash your Hands ~*

# MAKING PARTNER

## ~ *The person most interested in your Career is You* ~

One day, my boss, asked me to sit down for a review of my professional growth plan. This meant so much to me. It only took me the first nine years of my career, to realize I was the only person interested in my personal growth path, well let's just call it survival. I hadn't read Walt Mahler's book of advice yet, where this chapter's leading adage is derived. Walt stated "In most companies you will find only one person whom has a deep interest in your career, namely yourself." After our merger, we acquired a robust Human Resources group, which was often great and more often not so great. But this time it was great. I actually had an opportunity to make partner!

My first requirement I had already met. I had accepted a transfer to Atlanta, where I had an opportunity to build a bigger book of business to support my partner candidacy. My private life was difficult and moving to another city seemed like a safe, fresh way to make a new start. I loved my hometown of Philadelphia and would always be proud of my urban roots. Yes, as they say, you can take the girl out of Philly, but you can't take Philly out of the girl. Atlanta was my land of opportunity and adventure, but it still didn't feel like home.

*~ To grow might mean a Transplant*
*or at least a Pruning ~*

# ATLANTA TRANSPLANT

## ~ *Take time to Understand Others* ~

My girls were tiny, four and eight. When I made
the move to Atlanta, I wanted to communicate clearly
with them about their new home in images and terms
they could understand. From one of my business trips
to Atlanta I returned with postcards of the skyline, to
help Hannah and Chloe have a visual of their future
home.  Hannah wanted to know more about the house
and school hunting escapades, and could we get pets
in Atlanta.  Next, I went into Chloe's bedroom, the
four year old.  She nodded solemnly as I showed her
the pictures.

"But Mommy, I don't understand how we are
going to breathe."  Her childish lisp turned breathe
endearingly into Breeve.

"Whaddya mean Clo?"  I wasn't sure what she
was asking.

As she rolled her eyes in exasperation, "Mommy, how
are we going to breeve, when we are all living
underwater!"

Confused for a moment, a light went on and I replied, "Ohhhh, I seeee. I see why you were confused. No we are moving to Atlant-AAAA not Atlant-tisss. Atlant-tisss is the one underwater."

With a clear breath of relief, Chloe laughed and agreed to the move. How interesting, we had lots of Disney VCR tapes but not *Atlantis*. Where did she gain access to this mythological concept? Jarringly, I realized that if I hadn't stopped long enough to really listen, Chloe could have been having nightmares about drowning for the months leading up to the move, possibly fighting the move every step of the way.

*~ Really Listen.  Don't Assume.*
*Ask Questions. ~*

# TICKING OFF THE CHECKLIST

*~ How one journey can Change Everything ~*

There literally isn't time to breathe most days in public accounting world, so to have any time for reflection on one's own career was special. To Make Partner, the next item on my checklist was getting back to spending more time with clients, along with one thousand other things.

After my last promotion to manager, I spent more time in the office supervising and training the new associates. It wasn't as easy to spend time on the road dealing directly with clients, when there were staff members back in the office trying to prioritize their work product and waiting on my reviews and sign-offs.

Upon returning to clients, I would come to understand their bigger financial picture, and subsequently sell them more work as the end game. Juggling plates was an image coming to my mind. It all seemed so unattainable, but I loved the challenge of a new thing, so I was all for it. As a single mom, with a nanny, private school and a mortgage, a promotion would be welcome!

I mentally began plotting out where my clients lived, the ones that I didn't know so well, how could I optimize the most out of one trip, particularly to minimize time away from my young daughters. I looked at my address list from Kate's clients newly transitioned to me. I realized that a bunch of these were still my phone-only clients and lived in South Florida.

As a Philly girl, I went to the New Jersey shore for vacation, or sometimes had a special week in the Caribbean. I didn't want to go to Florida for anything, so my geography was quite vague. I knew Miami was on the tip and Orlando was somewhere in the middle, from my few obligatory trips to Disney. I also recalled that Florida was the idiotic state that caught the nation's attention with the hanging chad recounts in the Bush v. Gore Supreme Court decision. But that was the extent of my Floridian knowledge.

After spending an hour with a then new internet tool that you may recall, MapQuest, I figured out that about five of my current phone clients lived from Miami up to West Palm Beach, about an eighty-mile spread. By this time, I had driven each Friday from Philly to Lancaster. Upon my transfer to Atlanta, I spent most days driving around on the face of the clock, my nickname for the whimsical Atlanta layout, a groundhog day's experience if there ever was one. So, a little road trip didn't seem that daunting to me. But of course, trying to see five people in five different cities in 24 hours, wrapped around a plane trip, is was a bit over the top, even for me.

When I was sitting there with my map and ruler, I remember this feeling coming over me. It felt like this trip was very important and if I went through with it, I was going to change my life forever. I recall my reaction to this overwhelming feeling, "Come on now Erica, don't be so dramatic! Yeah, it's a big deal to try to 'make partner', but it's not all of that".

Little did I know, it was going to be a lot more than that. It WAS going to alter the fabric of everything. Because it was going to be the day I sat down across the table from Keith Elliott, The Voice, for the very first time.

*~ When the verbal becomes Physical
it can alter your Reality ~*

# PROSOPAGNOSIA

## ~ *When you can't see, Listen* ~

So, I started out with my usual shot gun method of throwing stuff at the wall to see what would stick. I picked out the forty-eight hours that worked for me to be away from home, about a month out. Then I called all of my phone clients that lived in Florida to tell them I would be in their neck of the woods for a few days and I would love to take them to lunch or dinner if they were in town and it worked for them.

"It would be great to be able to put a name with a face," I would say each time I hung up the phone. Which in most cases is normally true, but for me I had a secret physical disability that I worked really hard to camouflage. My facial recognition software was broken in my brain's computer. I can see the person's body and clothes, but in my memory bank it is as if someone took an eraser and rubbed out their face so there is just a blurry spot remaining.

Recall is especially difficult in a big group, when I'm making the rounds of introductions. If I am at an event, which normally requires people to wear similar things such as tennis uniforms, business suits, golf clothes or tuxedos, it can be unnerving. I found it quite disconcerting that everyone else seemed to recognize casual acquaintances with a brief glance at their face. It took a while for me to realize that I was the odd one. Upon this discovery, I began building my own supplementary skills to offset this embarrassing social disability.

First, I am very friendly with everyone at a party, as if we'd been friends for a while, because it was likely I had already met them once at that event! If I was wrong, I would rather error in that direction, because strangers often then did become friends. Two, I would try to look directly into the person's eyes. If we had met before, I would recognize the light of facial recognition in their eyes, and I could then respond accordingly. Surprisingly I found that people often veiled their eyes or intentionally misdirected their gaze, so it is actually more difficult than you think.

After completing my own research, to identify my disability and discover any possible remedies, I found I wasn't alone with this problem. The weakness even had its own medical diagnosis and of course an impossible to pronounce label: Prosopagnosia. After much phonetic practice, I finally could say it: Prah-so-pahhg-know-zhah. After two years of independent study of New Testament Greek that somehow counted as my two years of high school language, I did recall that proso came from the Greek word for face, so it was applicable. Prosopagnosia meant that one did not possess the "normal" eye to brain connection for successful facial recognition of other humans. That was me! I finally knew what was wrong with me.

There were actually documented cases that were significantly worse than my own, which was somehow sadly comforting, but there was no known remedy. The researchers had finally pinpointed the affected area in the brain, somewhere just above the medulla oblongata that was responsible for facial recognition, a tiny spot out of the whole brain. For people like me, it didn't fire up any neurons when presented with a face, unlike the rest of the world. No one really knew why, they were guessing at traumatic head injuries, but who can unravel all of the mysterious working of our unique minds and DNA. So, I was on my own, developing workarounds to navigate through social situations.

One of the strategies I developed to navigate the huge ocean of faces swimming around me, was to really listen to others. As we know, everyone's favorite most intimate subject matter is oneself. Starting as a young child, I began to ask grown-ups many questions. Asking them to tell me their stories. Initially, I used this device to hide the fact that I wasn't sure who I was talking to. Then I would use their responses to paste the face with the name and stories in my mental catalogue. Also, I could recall them from their voices and repeat their stories back to them in an emergency. This crutch for my own physical weakness grew into maybe my greatest strength. I learned to listen to people, really listen. While they were speaking, I studied all of their non-verbal gestures, mannerisms and linguistic habits. As a child, if I didn't know what the adult was actually talking about because it was over my head, I would listen to what was NOT being said. Often, I heard and saw the pain that was not verbally expressed. I knew what they meant, even when I had no idea what they were saying.

As I grew into an adult, listening served me well, because I became comfortable asking questions about subject matter that I knew nothing about. My curiosity only expanded all the more. And I learned a lot about many random topics. Over my young years, I learned another sad truth, no one is really listening to anyone else. There is a great human pain in this unconscious knowledge, because each of us has a deep need to have purpose in life, a relevancy. In today's world, there is a lot of poignant, digital screaming of "Look at me, look at me!" This is because each of us secretly knows that no one is listening to us, and it causes us to scream all the louder. When you learn to really listen to another, you are giving the greatest gift you can give, the gift of meaning.

When I was twenty-one and I accidentally entered the uber tax technical world of Big Four public accounting, I had little idea that my listening skills honed for surviving my own physical disability were going to be my greatest asset. When it came to listening to clients and co-workers, the clocks did stop, and I had all the time in the world to hear them. Of course, in the short run this was problematic when I had to piece together my two-week timesheet of billable hours. But in the long run it was priceless, because others KNEW that I was working hard to hear them, and looking for solutions to their problems. I was fascinated by what I heard, and I would come away from each conversation marveling at the complexity and depth of each human. In this way, I knew trust could actually grow as well as an understanding of each person. Trust was the cornerstone of my industry, no one is going to pay for advice, without it as a basis. Sadly, more often than not, I was sometimes the only one left listening to a particular soul. Over time, I came to see myself as a guardian-archivist of the human condition. One of my bosses would sometimes joke, that to be successful in our jobs we had to put on the proverbial clerical collar. I came to learn that there was truth in this. My listening skills brought spiritual depth to my career in taxes. Being the listening ear to others' pain brought me my own relevant purpose.

*~ Work on your Weakness and see what Emerges ~*

# MAKE PLAN

### ~ *Are you building Value*
### *or just wasting Time?* ~

I was even more anxious than normal about my timesheet during this quixotic quest for partnership. I was short on my normal chargeable hour goal again. I just finished up a wild call with a big-deal industrial executive. Suddenly fired, he had transformed himself into a NASCAR racing investor. He predicted how auto racing was going to be one of the biggest money sports of the future. Looking at his last tax return, I thought he had been around carbon monoxide for too long, but he certainly was a believer in his high-risk new adventure. Today, it shows what little I knew about this economic opportunity, as NASCAR is big business today.

After my head had cleared from the forest of tax attributes, claim of right doctrine and the deductibility of certain legal fees, I picked up the phone to call Keith next. We had to firm up our initial meeting date, place and time.

Keith seemed to have more time to talk than usual. As a recently retired executive, he was busy jetting around the world catching up on all the fun things he had missed. While working, his mind and body had been one hundred percent occupied with building corporate value and churning out earnings per share to keep the analysts and shareholders satisfied. Like all of us, even though retired, he still liked to actively participate as a contributing member of society. He served on a number of publicly held corporate board of directorships, as a well as a government think tank. He had just flown in from a board meeting, and was venting a bit about it on the phone with me.

If you listen to executives talk about their business plan for the quarter or year, they will identify both specific and broad goals. Incentive plans are paid out when management achieves these defined goals and therefore earned their related bonus. The shorthand expression is that the company had to "Make Plan" in order for management to receive their bonuses.

Keith complained, "I get really annoyed when I have to tell a CEO that Results Matter! I don't need to hear a lot of sad excuses about why he didn't make plan. And ahhh swear the bankers are the worst! They are like lemmings, following each other into the sea. They talk about how they have to pay more to recruit better talent away from their competitors. And I say, 'What talent? All of you bankers think alike. You haven't made a plan in years! As the chairman of the compensation committee, I'd have to be outta mah mind to approve that bonus package for management who hasn't made one plan presented to us!"

In a bit of a tither, Keith's southern drawl started to expand a bit from his normally more neutral speaking voice. As a middle manager myself, way down the line in a massive services firm, I found it fascinating to hear first-hand how the plan was created at the top of an organization. Our own firm's recent trend towards a business plan tied to a microscopic bonus package seemed quite contrived. Since the bonus was on average less than four percent of our annual salary, I wasn't making any life altering decisions with the money. I thought the minutia of my personal plan's goals were annoying in relationship to my possible bonus package. How much more blood could one stone give?

I re-focused in time to hear Keith continue, "I spent a lotta time trying to boil business principles down into Plain English. We ran a complicated business with a number of different segments that were hard to explain to our shareholders. For us to grow, we had to develop a clear message for our investors, employees, customers, vendors and the markets."

"In fact, that's what I called my first Annual Report that I was responsible for when I became CEO, *The Plain English of Shareholder Value.* I was proud that Israel Floyd, our company's lawyer, and I worked with the SEC to change the old legal language in the proxies to the Plain English style. I wanted more transparency for the investors, and ahhh felt like if we were all using Plain English, it wouldn't just be the lawyers that could read our reports."

"Wow!" was about all that I could muster. As someone that spoke to the IRS on a fairly regular basis, I couldn't contemplate getting one governmental body to do anything in the realm of changing their regulatory paper forest in any way whatsoever.

Keith charged forward, "In that first annual report I spelled out the four ways to create value for a company. I'll challenge any Business School Professor to name a fifth way. I-ahh spent a lot of time developing a Plain English framework to explain these concepts. Anything you can do as an executive or business owner to improve your company will fit into one of these four categories."

With that Keith quickly ticked off these four principles:

1. Make better what you already have

2. Get rid of stuff that doesn't work for you

3. Get more of the good stuff

4. Lower the Cost of Capital

How refreshingly simple but broadly applicable. Where had this man been my whole career? How much time had I wasted on stuff that should have been in the "get rid of" pile? Wow.

Upon my request, Keith promised to send me a copy of his old annual report, so I could spend more time digesting these broader concepts before our first meeting. I was a much better student of the written page, than oral lectures. If it wasn't in a story format, it was difficult for me to embed abstract concepts such as these from an oral form.

I was still trying to grasp the broadness of these principles, so I had to ask, "Well how does taxation fit into these categories? It is such a narrow field."

Without a second's thought, Keith replied, "Well Taxation could fit in a few ways, but definitely number four, Lower the Cost of Capital. When you reduce taxes to what is required to be paid, you increase net income, which increases owners' equity, which improves your debt to equity ratio. When you improve this ratio, you can borrow more, which will lower the cost of capital. Debt is cheaper than equity, for one thing because you can deduct the interest. Also, you maintain more control of your company because you aren't offering more shares to the public, as long as you don't borrow too much, so definitely number four, Lower the Cost of Capital."

I could tell he was smiling through his voice on the phone, which got me laughing a reply, "Wow I suddenly feel so much more important in what I do, than just pushing some papers around!"

With that we both laughed, confirmed our future date before we hung up. I drove home from work late that night, after wrestling my expense report into its virtual home. A small smile came to my face as I recalled and looked forward to the receipt of my first Plain English Annual Report of Shareholder Value. I wanted time to digest it, before I met the Voice. It was another piece in the R. Keith Elliott puzzle that my curious mind wanted to solve.

*~ When explaining delivered Value,*
*simple English is Best ~*

# ROAD TRIP

## ~ *Take time to Know your Customer* ~

First, I blew into Miami, the first stop on my personally derived magical mystery tour to quote The Beatles. I arrived for a brunch at Joe's Stone Crab, the famous Miami tourist joint. I met with my client, a plastic surgeon. He was the son of one of my entrepreneur clients. Now this was the early two-thousands before there were reality TV shows about facelifts. It was shocking to me, because the maître d', treated the Doc as if he was the mayor of Miami, and perhaps he was! As always, I enjoyed putting a face to a tax return, and begin to understand what motivated the person. Well, in my case, it was more like putting a story to a tax return, because it was quite likely I wouldn't recognize them the next time, unless they had some unique facial feature!

Working with multiple generations of a family unit is also fascinating, because every member has their own agenda and motivations, particularly when it came to money. It was an enjoyable lunch, especially because I was learning about a profession that I knew little about, so it was uncharted territory, my favorite kind.

As an aside, a real hero, was quietly sitting at a
table nearby. As a Philly Native, I recognized the
distinctive profile of our former Police Chief, John
Timoney. The lantern jawline was the thing that
registered with my broken facial recognition software.
Under Mayor Rendell, Timoney brought security back
to the streets of Philly. He had just taken a new job as
Miami's Police Chief. Since he noted the light of
recognition in my eyes, I gave him a subtle two finger
salute. Over the years in Philly, I recalled watching the
nightly news, where Timoney was often riding his
bicycle through the street at public events connecting
with the people. That chance glance reminded me that
yes taxes and surgery were important, but the safety
and security of our cities, was the thankless job that
really mattered.

$\sim$ *Remember What Matters* $\sim$

# ON TO BOCA RATON

## ~ *Take Alternative Paths and* *Enjoy the new Perspective* ~

Boca Raton, sounds so exotic, except perhaps if you're a Philadelphian with that nasally twang, and you pronounce it something like, "Bohhhhh-Kahhhhhh". Boca Raton literally means "the Mouth of the Rat". There is speculation that it is was originally the Spanish name for Biscayne Bay closer to Miami, perhaps it was a colloquial expression for a Thief's Inlet where illegal contraband could be traded.

Upon my initial arrival, my senses were overwhelmed with all the color: Azure blue skies, hot pink resort buildings, cobalt blue water glasses and emerald green putting greens. This is where one of my entrepreneurial client couples had finally retired. They had worked in tandem designing and selling distinctive stuffed animals creating an empire that was emotionally difficult to relinquish to their quite capable children's control.

It was when XM satellite radio was just founded, and the husband had fallen in love with the product and its stock. It seemed so exotic to think that the sky was the actual limit and one could listen to the same station no matter what state you called home. This was when you had to retro fit your car with an XM box, because it was so new.

The husband was showing off their beautifully built home and he trotted out one of the great couple jokes, "I gave my wife an unlimited budget to furnish our home, and she surpassed it". What kind of magical place was this Florida, where garages were fitted with spotless rubberized white floors?

As I continued my drive North to my dinner meeting with "The Voice Over the Phone" in Palm Beach, I picked up my Blackberry and tried calling a different client in Ft. Lauderdale again. This guy owed us a bunch on outstanding invoices. He had sold his share in a start up company, cashed out big. With the proceeds, he had bought a yacht that he was planning to offer on lease as his next business adventure. We had provided a lot of on point, sophisticated advice specific to his unique tax facts, and we hadn't been paid one dollar yet. Of course, he didn't answer, and I laughingly left a voicemail that I was in the neighborhood, would love to see the actual yacht and pick up a check if convenient.

Later, we ended up writing off 100% of these sophisticated fees, after a year of trying to collect. Today, Keith's pithy wisdom I know applies to this case: 'Whoever loses the least makes the most.' It was time to walk away and focus my energies elsewhere.

In the future, I would learn a lovely Keith-ism that I believe he learned from Walt Mahler:

*~ Swat Annoying Flies Early ~*

If I had met Keith earlier in life, there would have been a lot less flies around today. But better late than never.

# ARRIVING

*~ Remember there are many Others in your*
*Universe besides You ~*

I had some extra driving time before dinner, so I exited I-95 and drove up the coast on A1A, often with the ocean directly in view on my right. The next morning, I was going to fly out of the West Palm Beach airport back to Atlanta. I mused to myself, "What is West Palm Beach doing over here on the East coast of Florida next to the Atlantic Ocean?"

I found out the Why, later that evening, when I entered the iconic Town of Palm Beach, straining the boundaries of its intercoastal island shores. The Town of Palm Beach was the center of its own universe, similar to Beverly Hills which is adjacent to the City of Los Angeles yet clearly separate. The beautifully appointed Palm Beach had the City of West Palm Beach at its Western back and the endless ocean stretching towards the Eastern horizon at its front door. Therefore, the name West Palm Beach was aptly named, at least in a Copernican geo-centric way, if you were a Palm Beach-er.

My usual fashion is to arrive in a new town with a general cartographical, aerial assessment stored in my brain. Then I drive myself around to see how well I can find what I was looking for (to quote U2) independent of any navigational help. It seemed to heighten my senses, and I got a better residual picture of the streets to file away inside my head.

As the sun was setting in the West, I recall turning a corner and seeing the infamous Palm Beach County Courthouse looming in front of me. It was where our country learned together that a chad was a technical voting term. It was no longer just a boy's name or a country in Africa. A chad was a failing appendage of a U.S. voting ballot, which altered the course of America's politics due to the approximate 538 clinging chads that refused to be properly punched and separated from their ballots. It was also the courthouse where infamous trials took place. You may recall that the Kennedy Smith rape was some of the first accidental C-SPAN reality TV show viewing, for God's sake.

Yes, here too, a dark shadow lived behind the beautiful palms and dazzling foliage. It wasn't all Florida sunshine, there was drama and silent suffering as we know accompanies all walks of life. Here amidst the beauty, the wounds were just better disguised.

~ *Experience the Moment* ~

# WE SAT FOR DINNER

## ~ *Follow the Trail of your Instincts* ~

Florida was SO flat and wide open. Any large trees, even the iconic palms, were imports and not related to the indigenous scrubby Florida Pine. Streets were laid out in grids, no macadam mimicry of meandering ancient cow paths down an old hill side, because there is no grass and there are no hills. As I pulled into the back entrance of the parking lot for the Palm Beach Grill, I looked around the carefully manicured contrived space. It was a perfect night, with no rain.

As I ripped open the door of my little rental car to punch my social time clock right on the number, I noticed this young college boy running towards me. He was dressed in a valet's uniform. This was quite a foreign experience for me back in Philly, to quote Will Smith. Or as Genesis sang, one could stand alone in the rain for hours, before a valet maybe appeared to take your keys at some point in time. And if one chose to pay for his services, one could wait for a very long time before your car reappeared, perhaps still intact, perhaps not. A valet was normally a stress inducing event for me. I didn't have time to waste waiting around for someone to do something for me that I could do myself but faster.

But by coming in the back door, these alert valets thought I was trying to cheat them out of a tip, by parking myself. It was then I realized I had fallen down a rabbit hole, and was in some fairy land, where valets wanted to park your car six spaces away from the front door on a Van Gogh-ian Starry Night. And people actually wanted to tip them for this! Where was the pixie dust? I must follow this mysterious trail to its magical source.

I am quite tall for a woman, almost six feet in my bare feet. When I walked into the Palm Beach Grill, the bar was packed from the entrance all the way down to the back wall. Standing in my heels, I looked over the sea of heads before me, and it was then I realized, I didn't know what The Voice actually looked like. I wasn't expecting to sort through this mass of cocktail humanity. But at that moment, I looked into the eyes of a stranger, that somehow were also the eyes of my oldest, dearest friend, for these were the eyes of R. Keith Elliott.

I couldn't help myself, as I broke into this huge grin. Keith's fair skin turned pink, as he laughed and laughed, as I walked towards him. As I weaved through the wave of humanity, I could see that Keith and I were on the same eye level. His fair Scottish skin and hair, flickered amber in the dimmed lighting. His shoulders, were draped in a navy- blue sports jacket, what I came to later know as the Palm Beach uniform. But those shoulders were like a coat rack with a broad swimmer's back stretched in between. Even though officially retired, it looked like he'd be comfortable striding across some Scottish moor to wrestle an antlered deer to the ground with his bare, burly hands.

Keith had brought his closest friend, Hamlin, along for the meeting. They were having a raucous, joyous time already. It looked like Hamlin slapped Keith on the back in some kind of congratulatory gesture.

So, I must say it wasn't until a few years later that I learned what words actually passed between Hamlin and Keith, on this precipitous occasion. Apparently, Keith had already liked what he had heard over the phone, and then liked what he saw when he looked into my eyes. He was much more engaged then he let on. As Keith had turned towards me, he had leant over and whispered into his friend's ear, "Hamlin, my boy, from here on out, it is all about execution!"

When I reached them both, Keith introduced me to Hamlin as his tax advisor. Hamlin shook my hand and jokingly said my personal tag line, "But you don't look like a tax accountant!"

Now as you already know, I have heard this a few times. In the beginning, I was very self-conscious about this "you don't look like you belong" comment.

But by then, I could take it in stride responding with a look of surprise, "But THIS is my disguise!" as I waved my hand around to emphasize the body that I had snatched from a real human.

Thus, began my life's grandest adventure. Hamlin faded away in a gentleman-like fashion to one of the many other bars in town. Much later, I would find out what a dear, close friend Hamlin really was. But that night, Keith and I sat for hours telling each other stories from our lives, as if we were catching up at an alumni reception. So new and exotic, yes. But somehow poignant in what we had missed.

When I realized that Keith was still having a hard time recovering from the fact that a regular looking person could actually be an accountant, I started to get a little nervous. I thought it was probably the right time to pull out the two dear little pictures of my young daughters where Kindergarten was the only familial graduation achieved by this point in time.

But working career women with young children didn't seem to phase this wrecking ball in the least. He placed his two thick fingers on the frames and said, "They are beautiful just like their mother." I took a deep breath and muttered one of my favorite euphemisms, "Oh My Word."

Desperately, I searched for a way to change the focal point to Keith. I asked him to tell me his best business experience, he was very quick to say, "It was with Terence in South Africa".

Immediately, my mind went to the iconic movie scene of sprawling African Savannahs with a Meryl Streep voice over murmuring, "I once had a farm in Africa."

But in my personal version, the national anthem of my teenage youth echoed between my ears as Keith's stories unwound. Toto began to sing their iconic crossover hit: "It's gonna take a lot to drag me away from you…gonna take some time to do the things we never had…"

With a little sigh, I secretly began to wish it could be true. But it was way too late, somehow the two of us had just kept missing each other, one intersection at a time.


~ *Listen to Yourself* ~

# THE BIGGEST DEAL
# OF MY LIFE

*~ Collaboration leads to Creation ~*

"It was when I was the CFO at Engelhard, way back in the 1980's," said Keith.

"Wow, I would have guessed it was after you left Engelhard. I would think your last job as CEO of Hercules would've been it!"

"No, that would be a fair guess, because there were a lot of events that were definitely a LOT more challenging as CEO. Tom tried to tell me that when he retired, but I didn't believe him until I went through the experience myself. Ever since the day I became CEO, I've never slept the same since. When you know that every business decision you make affects the lives and future pension benefits of thousands of employees, you never rest the same again."

"But no. My Platinum deal with Terence Wilkinson at Lonrho Platinum in South Africa was the biggest deal of my business career, the best. And it was the most rewarding in Terence's career too. I say the best because the business arrangement we conceived, collaborated on and executed in the 1980's is still kicking today, employing thousands of South African Miners and supplying platinum group metals to the world, and we are both long gone from those business ventures. But I have to explain the why we needed to make the deal, it was because we at Engelhard had invented a new catalytic converter that increased the world's demand for platinum group metals. Our scientists had invented a new formula derived from platinum-based chemistry that made the thing work."

## ~ Never Fear a New Formula ~

# MEETING IN THE LADIES' ROOM

*~ Develop yourself, you will naturally*
*Attract positive Interest ~*

On this dizzying note, I felt it was time to rest my brain cells, which felt like they were going to explode. It had been a long car ride and I hadn't had time to freshen up yet. I called for a cerebral time out with a much-needed trip to the loo.  I wandered down the long golden lit, sparkling granite hall, to the dark mahogany door of the plush ladies' restroom.  As I found my way to a stall, I noticed two ladies of a certain age.  They had hair colors that I could only liken to tropical birds of paradise.  They wore more make up then I've worn in a year, yet were applying even more engine-red lipstick to their permanently stained mouths.  They were comparing notes about which restaurant was the next best stop in town. Preferring a place disturbingly called the Leopard Lounge which offered Two-Fer-One cocktails, and had the most available men on a Tuesday night.

The women's social strategizing reminded me of one of my favorite Freestyle dance hits. Klymaxx's 1985 recording started playing, "I got a meeting in the ladies' room. Be back real soon." I was a closet freestyle dance music lover. It was one of the earliest forms of electronic dance music that was popular with the Italian and Puerto Rican communities in Philly and New York City. As you can imagine, not many in my accounting or church circles even knew that this genre existed. I had to search pretty hard to locate a set of CDs which I kept in my car's CD auto changer.

I smiled and rolled my eyes as I heard them exit the bathroom, chirping away with who would call whom if one of them met Mr. Right. After a couple hours in this town's bar, I recognized a dramatic social shift compared to other places. There were many, many attractive older available females relative to the number of older men in this town. It seemed to create an extra level of desperation among some of these women, that the only way they were going to remain desirably relevant was to fight for a man, no holds barred.

As I walked back to our seats at the bar, I realized Keith was in trouble, and actually had a small look of terror on his face, when his eyes met mine. The same two tropical biddies- had seized the opportunity of seeing Keith alone at the bar. One had actually jumped into my seat, and they each had one of their arms linked through his, in a technical armlock. Wow, I was living out lyrics that Klymaxx was still crooning in my head, how surreal.

One of them was cooing in his ear, "What are you up to tonight? You are just like a little gumdrop sitting here all by yourself."

I couldn't help enjoying a bit of Keith's clear level of discomfort. Turn-about is fair play I chuckled to myself, as I recalled years of vulgar cat calls from bored construction workers as I hurried down the streets of Philly trying to grab a quick lunch. Suddenly, I found it quite endearing that my opinion of him, actually mattered to this titan of industry. At the same time, I felt a level of pity for these emotionally desperate women. Lastly, a brief flash of relief, that thank God there was somewhere in the world where men were the target. A smug sense of relief washed over me, as my cloak of invisibility felt like a talisman of protection. Generally, the men seemed to be on the defensive, overwhelmed by a quiet bombardment of a feminine "pick me" game. But yet, it was Keith clearly showing his hand of intention to me, as I shivered a quick recognition of delight.

Keith, always the southern gentleman, said, "Ladies, I am sorry to disappoint, but I am having dinner with my tax advisor tonight. Let me introduce you to her. Erica this is April and Nancy."

With an appalling glare, brief nod and a sniff of the well powdered nose, April flounced off and left Nancy to deal with me.

"Well you don't look like MY tax advisor. I have a lot of race horses, so I need an expert from one of the big firms in New York," Nancy launched the first shot.

Feigning friendship, I replied, "Oh, this is what I wear when they let me out of the office! But seriously, that's great to hear you have expert advice, because horses are tricky tax animals." The pun was lost on Nancy here. I couldn't help getting a bit catty and decided I would show off some of my horse taxation knowledge.

"But I do know what you mean, I have some horse clients too, at the Big Four Firm where I work. If you are careful with the depreciable lives of horses when they convert from racing to breeders, you can really marry up cash flow and the benefit of tax losses in certain years. As described in Revenue Procedure 87-56, breeders have a seven-year depreciable life for regular tax purposes, while racehorses have a three-year depreciable life. But regardless, the awesome thing about depreciating horses is that it can create an ordinary business loss on paper that can possibly offset other active income. Of course, this depends on your personal facts and circumstances such as the amount of time you actively commit to your serious business of racing."

At this point, Nancy decided I was definitely a competitor pissing in her backyard, and a problem that needed to be eliminated. I couldn't stop laughing inside. She was determined to finagle her way into our bar set up, to ensure that the riff raff (me) didn't mistakenly win the attentions of one of her "horses in the stable".

Keith replied with all the seriousness he could muster, "I'm sorry Nancy but we still have not covered all of our business matters at this time, so perhaps another time?"

With that veiled look only possible from underneath a cobra's hooded eyes, Nancy slid down the bar to another potential prey. What worm hole did I slip through? How did I get here?

*~ Humor can be Body Armor too ~*

# CARL'S SECRET SCIENCE PROJECT

*~ Don't give up with Tinkering,*
*who knows what you may Invent ~*

When we returned to our private tête-à-tête, I wanted to pick up the conversational thread about business wheeling and dealing in South Africa with Terence. My mind was so fired up, I wanted to know everything.

"At the time I joined Engelhard, the company's scientists had already invented the chemical process that ran a catalytic converter. This single invention changed the global relationship of the world's platinum supply and demand at the time. There were no longer enough platinum group metals to go around based on the world's existing mining capabilities. The metal was there deep underground, but there had been no significant increase in demand to require a new mine to go and get it. Mines are expensive endeavors to build and operate, it requires a long-term demand before even considering opening a new mine."

I was still back at the surprising concept that somewhere there was platinum embedded in my car. I asked, "You mean there is platinum in my car? I had no idea! What's the catalytic converter do?" I was pleased to have a vague car relationship in mind, but that was all that I could come up with on the fly. Right away, one of the things I liked about Keith was he didn't make you feel dumb for asking curious questions that one knew nothing about.

With a smile Keith said, "Would you like a small lesson on the catalytic converter?" As I grinned and nodded my head, he continued, "At the time, there was a bunch of scientific research saying that the carbon monoxide (CO) molecule was creating a hole in the ozone layer. Platinum group chemistry was utilized to help solve this environmental problem, if chemists could convert the CO molecule to CO2, water and hydrogen gas, it would be a more natural molecule, that trees could eat and convert back to oxygen."

I was picturing this beautiful forest of trees, covered in moss, and some kind of red checked table coverlet with Hansel & Gretel-like bread crumbs leading the way out of the dark forest, pumping out oxygen for us all to breathe. The two of us were cuddled up quite cozily continuing this conversation at our own private picnic. I could hear Keith's voice calling to me like a siren from the edge of the abyss. What was he saying? All I could feel was the hypnotic vibration of his voice.

"So, a catalytic converter cylinder has interior surface that is covered with honeycomb-like structures. The cylinder itself is about eight inches long and similar in diameter to a large grapefruit. Then, the cylinder is dipped into a suspension or a mixture of platinum group metals and an adhesive. The mixture adheres to the interior surfaces of the catalytic converter. The entire thing is then encased in stainless steel which is then seated in the exhaust system of a car. The catalytic converter is in the center of the casing, so there is room around it. The exhaust from the car's manifold is forced into one end of the catalytic converter. As the exhaust passes over the honeycombed surface of platinum group metals, those metals cause a chemical conversion of the exhaust gases from carbon monoxide (CO) to carbon dioxide or $CO_2$ and water."

I had flashbacks of pictures of the periodic table on this black page of a text book that Mr. Bacon expected us to memorize in Introduction to Chemistry in eleventh grade. I loved Biology but NOT Chemistry! I hated such things as atomic weight and mass, and what made them different! I much preferred dissecting frogs and fetal pigs. I especially found it difficult to recall these chemical elements, while I was having a cocktail! I rarely drank. Basically, because I didn't trust how men behaved around me sober, let alone drinking. Yet somehow, I felt safe with this man.

Keith continued, "I got to talk with Carl Keith, the leading Engelhard scientist, responsible for inventing the latest version of the catalytic converter. I asked him, 'How did you do it?'".

"Carl told me there were at least three different times during his tenure at Engelhard, where management 'deep sixed' it, because they had to prioritize the budget and this idea was stubbornly remaining only an idea. Carl was having trouble coaxing it into the physical, so the research costs were not yet paying off. Carl knew he was onto something and he didn't want to quit, due to monetary restrictions, so each time he would hide money in his corporate operating budget. That way he could secretly continue his research on the new chemistry. It took him about two hundred thousand a year to keep the research alive, which was a pretty small budgetary line item at the time."

"So, when Carl and his fellow scientists discovered these latest catalytic converter technologies, it created a whole new global demand, that tapped out the current market supply of platinum group metals. The technological jump in chemistry created a huge jump in clean air, but this discovery was dependent on platinum. And platinum was a hugely labor-intensive endeavor and it was only found in certain parts of the globe."

I interrupted, "So do you (or in my brand of slang 'Soh-duh-ya') mean that for example we haven't discovered that much platinum here in America?" I continued to muse, "I know I read a book about the copper kings in Montana I think, and obviously the gold rush out West, but I don't recall ever hearing anything about platinum on our continent. Huh. I never really thought about this before."

Keith smoothly continued, "Yes, that's exactly right. And this is how I got to South Africa, it is one of the richest sources of platinum group metal ore bodies in the world today. Russia would be second, but their reefs are less rich in platinum itself, so they exert a lot more effort to extract less platinum at the end of the day."

"Rustenburg sold all the metal to us at Engelhard that they could. But it wasn't enough anymore based on Carl's scientific discovery. It was the game changer. Rustenburg was owned by Harry Oppenheimer.

"Wait a minute, THE Harry Oppenheimer?" I interjected.

"Yes, that's the one." Keith smiled sardonically.

"Harry was our major supplier of our resource requirements, but he was also our most serious investor. Based on that I had to go see Harry first before I started courting other suppliers."

*~ Curiosity is a Powerful Trait,*
*question Everything ~*

# HARRY OPPENHEIMER
# AND SOUTH AFRICA

*~ Ensure backers agree with a big Change of*
*Course, so you Maintain their Confidence ~*

I asked, "What? You met with Harry
Oppenheimer? And how was he both your supplier
and owner?" Now when Keith answered this question
that night, it was difficult for me to grasp all of it from
his oral explanation. As the CPA side of my brain
required, Keith graphed out on a paper napkin for me
to be able to visualize the structural elements.

And so, Keith began, "This is how I understood
it, because I wasn't a member in Anglo American, the
largest platinum supplier on the planet. Anglo was a
Harry Oppenheimer company. Through it, Harry
owned a big piece of us at Engelhard. It was large
enough that he earned three board seats on our board
of directors.

But we were also his customer through one of
his other subsidiaries which was called Rustenburg.
But fundamentally this was the thing, Harry's
conglomerate, E. Oppenheimer & Sons of South
Africa, owned thirteen percent of EACH of their

various business investments. Harry's father Ernest started it all. I only knew the son, Harry, who invested in so many different companies. He was such a gentleman."

Still amazed, I said, "What do you mean he was a gentleman?"

"I don't remember when this exactly occurred, but on one of many business trips to South Africa, I had the privilege of having dinner at Mr. Oppenheimer's home. I know it was early in my South African travels, because the hotel where I stayed was in Johannesburg and not out in the suburbs. This meant that Johannesburg was a lot safer, so the timing would have put it somewhere before 1985."

"I literally arrived on the airplane after flying overnight from London around nine a.m. I had unpacked my suitcase and had gotten a really good nap for about four hours to catch up on sleep. When I woke up, I called Hank Slack's home phone number, because I had a few work questions for him.

Now Hank was Harry Oppenheimer's son-in-law, and he served Harry as his right-hand man, personal assistant. Mary was Harry's daughter's name. She had been married a few times, so Hank was her current husband. Hank was originally from New Jersey, so it was somewhat natural for him to be one of Harry's representatives on our board of directors at

Engelhard.  Our headquarters were in New Jersey too."

It was known that the role as Harry's personal assistant was a jumping off point for potential high performers in Harry's organizations.  Kind of a keep 'em close and train 'em up."

I started musing about a book my sister gave me to read.  It was about the families that were serious founders then donors to New York's Metropolitan Museum of Art.  One of the women along the way had definitely been Mrs. Charlie Engelhard.  I started giggling thinking about how New Yorkers always think of themselves as owning the world, in my Philly chip on my shoulder attitude.  Isn't it just fitting that one of the Met's biggest donors was being controlled by South Africa?  Wait, I was missing a funny part of Keith's story.

"Mary answered my phone call instead of Hank and informed me that Hank was out of the country on business.  Then I was surprised when she asked me if I had any plans for dinner, 'because I need a man tonight.  Will you be me my date to my mother's home for dinner?'  I was a little unsettled determining how to respond to Harry's daughter.  I was concerned, because I knew that Harry was a very traditional, proper gentleman, which included wearing black tie every night for dinner.  I didn't have any evening clothes, since I was traveling on business, I just had a dark suit." (Who doesn't travel half way around the world without a tuxedo?)

Mary said, "Well I need to call my Mother and ask permission." After a few moments Mary returned my call confirming that her mother was perfectly fine with making an exception that evening for my suit and tie. Mary said she would pick me up at the front of the hotel. I went down from my room and was standing just outside the front entrance of the hotel. When she drove up in a BMW convertible with the top down, I walked over to get into the car. I felt like I was in a James Bond movie, there was Mary who wore a fancy cocktail dress, with a hemline just below where it needed to be. How did a little boy with a paper route from the back woods of South Carolina come half way around the world to this moment?" Keith said shaking his head in disbelief.

"We drove to Brenthurst, Harry's beautiful twenty-five-acre estate right in the middle of downtown Johannesburg. After dinner, the men would have cigars. But even with all of this formal tradition, all the men would go out into the garden and have a pee on the lemon tree."

"What? Do you mean like Anthony Hopkins did in *The World's Fastest Indian*? Is that an actual thing? Seems quite over the top doesn't it?" as I mused on my normal meal when I got home from work in the dark, dining alone on Rice Chex when the rest of the world was asleep.

Enjoying the humorous movie parallel, Keith continued, "Also, no one cares to remember this today, but when Apartheid was still going in South Africa, Harry was a leader of the vanguard in their Parliament to vote Yes for 'One Man, One Vote.' It took a while for the rest of his fellow politicians to catch up with Harry."

"Wow. Hmmm. Maybe, I'm thinking because of Harry's vast empire, he could vote as he thought, because no one could push him around so easily? He couldn't be bought," I surmised.

With a thoughtful look, Keith responded, "That's a way to look at it. But to continue with the ownership structure, here's the thing, each of Harry's investments owned 38% of each other. So, when Harry added together his ownership percentage of E. Oppenheimer & Sons in the individual business investments, in total he owned 51% of everything. This unique arrangement made it possible for each company to also be listed on a public stock exchange, otherwise called a terminal market. Therefore, each of Harry's companies had a value set by a public market price for everything that he owned for every day. In essence, he had a privately controlled conglomerate with a public stock market price. Anglo-American was the centerpiece of Harry's empire. A small part of it was DeBeers, the diamond producer and seller. You may have heard of them," Keith said with a wry smile.

"That was the little part?" I found that hard to put in perspective, after a life time of being bombarded with black velvet back drops in "diamonds are forever" DeBeers commercials. And this is where Keith was busy with his pen and ink cocktail napkin drawing of Harry's ingenious corporate structure.

Keith continued, "Yes. Anglo American was the big deal. Its principal product was gold plus its investments in other companies. So you know the James Bond movies and the character Goldfinger right? It is said by some that Goldfinger was based on Oppenheimer and some say it was Engelhard. Probably the character was based a bit on both men."

"Anyways, among the businesses that Harry owned and operated was Rustenburg Platinum, which at that time was and probably still is the largest platinum group metal company in the world. Where in all of this empire fell the remaining businesses, I am not sure, but they included breweries, railroads, forests, paper making companies, and distilleries."

Now lost in my own forest of corporate entities, I asked, "So, how did Harry own a piece of Engelhard?"

At this point, I wasn't able to think anymore in corporate chart structures. I was looking at the muscular set of Keith's shoulders, and his tranquility while speaking about globe-trotting escapades, while sipping on Scotch. I noticed how he hooded his eyes to mask his feelings, as was required to survive corporate boardroom warfare I'm sure. I wondered what it would take to forge a bond of trust with such a man. Irrationally I though, yes, a man whom I would jump off a cliff for, at minimum miss a plane for. Would he even notice?

With a sphinxlike smile that seemed to hold a million secrets, Keith continued, "Yes, in a round-about way, Harry owned a piece of us. Minorco was a company controlled by Oppenheimer based in Bermuda. Initially, Minorco owned 27% of Engelhard. He also owned a piece of Johnson Matthey, who was our competitor when it came to the automobile catalytic converter business."

It must have been some kind of premonition, I now know. I saw us on the Suez Canal, walking through the Valley of the Kings, down the Avenue of the Sphinxes, just like in Agatha Christie's *Murder on the Nile*. Then I snapped back to the present moment.

I replied, "Ahhh, so you basically had to ask permission of your backer, before going and courting another supplier, the Catch-22. And how 'Cain and Abel' of Harry to own a piece of both of world's major supplies to the auto industry!" I couldn't help interjecting with a bit of sarcasm. But then more thoughtfully I continued, "But I guess in the end it behooved Harry to root for your success. For when you succeeded, he did too."

Keith concluded, "Ironically, Carl's automobile invention became a cash cow for Engelhard in a few different ways. The invention he had had to quietly keep working on, of his own volition. Yes, Harry at Anglo American was our main supplier, but Johnson Matthey, his other investment and customer was first in line. They were already his biggest distributer of Rustenburg metals to the world. Harry always honored his contracts and his word, being the gentleman that he was."

*~ Think how to turn Adversity*
*into mutual Success ~*

# VERTICAL INTEGRATION

### ~ *Watch and Work for Magical Connections* ~

"So, did you get to meet with Mr. Oppenheimer any other times?" I asked Keith.

He replied "Well, I know one other time was when we were interested in making a bid for Mallinckrodt."

I couldn't help interrupting to phonetically sound out the foreign sounding name, *Mallon-crott* ?

"Yes, Mallinckrodt was a specialty chemical company located in St. Louis, Missouri, that most people probably never heard of. But it did invent the formula for acetaminophen, which you would know as Tylenol. After they formulated the acetaminophen powder, they sold it to McNeil Labs who then produced and distributed Tylenol. At the time it was public information that Avon had approached Mallinckrodt, they were interested in buying it."

"Ya mean, Avon the wholesale makeup company?" I asked incredulously.

Keith nodded and continued, "One of my key principles that I relied upon when I was considering an acquisition was try to understand the Why they wanted to sell. Very often it was a load of horsesh*t. Maybe they wanted to off load bad sh*t off their balance sheet onto someone else, like product liabilities or future pension benefits. You have to be careful about what you buy, because it can come back and bite you in the a$$."

With another smile, Keith continued, "We took a look at the possible Mallinckrodt-Engelhard Combination and it was a pretty good strategic mix. We didn't want to lose out to Avon. We could've kept looking long and hard to find such a good combination for ourselves. Mallinckrodt had different specialty chemical products then us, quite complimentary in fact. They were a good financial mix too. We decided we wanted to be a bidder. Therefore, we had to go and talk to our effective thirty percent owner, which was Mr. Oppenheimer. We asked him if he would participate at his ownership level, if we needed to sell shares to raise more money to make the purchase. So, my boss and CEO at the time, and I presented the case to the Anglo-American board at Harry's South African Headquarters. It was the last item on the agenda before lunch and we were asked to meet the board members in the chairman's dining room. When we got there, our personal name tags were at each place setting. Harry was sitting at one end of the table, and we were seated on opposite sides of him. Harry came in fifteen minutes later and said 'Well, you have your money, so now go win.'"

"We sure tried! But as it turned out Avon was willing to pay a stupid price, so we decided to back out. Avon bought Mallinckrodt at that inflated price and it eventually almost bankrupted Avon. They wanted the acquisition, because of the concept of vertical integration: in essence they could own the fragrance making business that they required in their own products. But in the end, they had no idea (Keith's drawl made it sound more like ahhhh-dee-ahh which was so more pleasant on my ear) how to manage a chemical plant and it didn't work. They had to spin Mallinckrodt back out to save themselves which made Mallinckrodt independent again. I've always been a value buyer, and this was a clear example of why."

"Whaddya mean a vertical integration?" I asked.

Keith responded with, "Well a perfect Vertical Integration, for mah money, would be, we own the mine, the refinery, the company that makes the converter, the exhaust company the car manufacturer and the distributer. You would own from the raw material all the way to the end product and consumer. Of course, in real life this doesn't happen often, but if you can get close, it's magical." As Keith warmed to his dual Subject Matter Expertise on both Chemistry and Economics, his subtle Southern draw expanded as he continued, "But in real life it doesn't always work out thah way. You can own a bunch ah tha pieces, but only if you don't lose your mahnnnd and overpay for stuff."

Inwardly I sighed, for I could listen to this silky hybrid of speech for a long time. I loved hearing these complex MBA concepts boiled down into succinct, simple definitions, in Keith's soft sexy spellbinding dialect.. I kicked myself again for going to the small liberal arts college for my desired business degree, when I was unsure that my academic and religious family would be that supportive of pursuing a career in business. But back to the abstract theories being birthed into more visual pictures before my eyes, I was hungry for more.


~ *Don't pay a Stupid Price, it can kill You* ~

# TERENCE

## ~ *Keep talking to develop a New,* *mutually Profitable Method* ~

"So, let's get back to you, Terence and the global platinum supply. How did you and Terence actually get going on the new deal?" I asked.

"Well my company, Engelhard couldn't get all the platinum we needed from Oppenheimer anymore, after Carl's discovery with the catalytic converter ratcheted up the new level of demand. Johnson Matthey got all of Oppenheimer's platinum it wanted from Anglo American, since they were already the world's largest distributor of industrial use platinum group metals, before our new discovery. They had this rock-solid agreement with Oppenheimer to get all the platinum group metals that they mined. And mind you, Harry owned a piece of both of us, so he wanted both of our companies to win. Oppenheimer got our platinum allotment increased to Four hundred and ninety-five thousand ounces, but it still wasn't enough to meet our new demand. There was a period when Engelhard was forced to buy metal from a bunch-a places: Rustenburg, Impala (another South African company), the communist Russian government, one small mine in Colorado and what was then a relatively small South African mining business named Lonrho Platinum.  And this was how I forged a business relationship with Terence, the entrepreneur and CEO at Lonrho.  It was borne out of the world's need for cleaner burning automobiles.

We had the new formula, but we need the raw materials to produce the new product."

*~ Adversity opens our Eyes to new Methods ~*

# HOW CAN WE MAKE IT THAT NO ONE CAN LOSE?

### ~ *Balance Pride with Compassion* ~

As Keith continued to talk, I started looking at his strong hands, and how calm they remained on the table, as he spoke. I thought of my partial Italian DNA aspect that seemed to live on a hare trigger every time my mouth opened. My arms would elevate of their own accord and my hands would start waving above my head.

I wanted to "Stop All The Clocks" to quote W. H. Auden and listen to Keith's mellifluous voice tell yarns forever. In the space between my ears, Toto's hypnotic refrain started up again, "I guess it rains down in Africa, we're gonna take some time to do the things we never had" I couldn't help but hum and sing along under my breath. Did I really have to fly back to the real world tomorrow?

"Come again? What? Wait a minute, so I have a question. So how did you and Terence make this happen?"

Keith continued, "I guess it started at Platinum Week, which was held in London once a year. I was there when sometime around 1982 we formed the Platinum Association which was a combination of users and producers. At one point I was president of the thing."

"That is so weird!" I said in eighties' valley girl vernacular. "In 1982, I remember putting our boom box on the floor of the gym, and listening to 'Africa' by Toto as my high school basketball team ran wind sprints! And you were actually down in Africa," I murmured more to myself.

Keith said, "I love that song too. It is one of my favorite songs ever. In 1988, I got the call from Pat Retief, the president of JCI and the Platinum Association. 'Keith, we would like for you to be the big speaker at the Savoy Hotel dinner'. It was the real deal! One thousand people attended this dinner from around the world. You would come through the doors. An actual Beefeater dressed in full regalia would bang his big staff upon the floor. Then he would say something like, 'Mr. and Mrs. Keith Elliott of Engelhard'."

With a quiet pause, and bowed head, "Often, I had to go by myself. And sometimes Terence was there by himself, along with a bunch of people from South Africa." Later I learned what secret sorrows were hidden behind this comment.

Wistfully, I looked at Keith's mouth as he continued to spin these tales of globe-trotting, business acumen. Inexplicably, a small voice inside me said, "If it had been me, you would have never walked into that room alone, if I could've helped it." What the heck was happening to me? I shook my head to try to clear this disconcerting mental commentary.

"I even recall what I talked about that night. I intended it to be controversial I can tell you that. The Russians, Impala, and a whole lotta other people knew we were working on a growth plan. I gave them the formula for what I thought was a legal, sensible approach for the platinum industry to set as a standard as a whole. It was important to do things the right way, so we didn't commit any wrongful acts such as price fixing. Since we were expanding the industry's overall supply, we should announce our public intention to increase capacity about a year ahead of time that we were putting into place. It allows the market sufficient time to set a price. If all the mines try to rush through the door at the same time, it will definitely suppress the price and hurt all of us. If we did it one at a time, we are all so much better off, because the price will stay higher, and your existing facilities will be so much more profitable."

"If each company could increase their capacity on a controlled basis, we could all survive instead of just a few. Other mines started saying they had to increase capacity too, because they didn't want to be left behind. So, my speech was focused on a coordinated public effort to sanely increase capacity. It is better to be concerted in the industry's efforts. The world's platinum demand was growing exponentially because of the greenhouse gas cutting catalytic converter. We needed the entire industry to stay healthy and profitable, so we could provide the world's supply. It had already happened in the paper industry, they have this big investment in machines, so when the price of paper goes down, everyone gets scared. Everyone starts running their massive one quarter of a mile long (I know hard to imagine!) machines faster. It feels counter-intuitive to slow down production and stabilize the industry's price."

"This was basic economic principles, but everyone isn't an economist, and everyone doesn't have the nerve to slow down and do it the right way. Short term fears drive people to make stupid economic decisions."

Keith finished, "To my recollection, it was at one of these early on annual conferences that Terence and I started really talking seriously about our big deal. It was only an idea then. From idea to a signed contract, was about two and a half years from start to finish. Then it was about another two full years for Terence's team to expand, build and acquire three mines, respectively."

I swore I could see a slight mist cloak Keith's eyes as he quietly said, "At the end, it was my proudest business moment, because our partnership created a lot of new jobs. I would estimate about fifteen thousand South African miners were put to work because of our deal. Plus add on seven people on top of that, which was the average family size there, so we helped house, feed and clothe about one-hundred and twenty thousand people overall. Those mines and jobs still exist today some thirty years later."


*~ Take your Time to do things the Right Way ~*

# PARALLEL LIVES IN THE EIGHTIES

## ~ *Separate Lives, but Similar Paths* ~

Suddenly, I connected Keith's South African timeline to my own high school life in the mid-eighties. Our lives were nowhere close to crossing yet, they were running parallel courses for a while still to come. While Keith's business life was immersed in South Africa, this divided country was just entering the fringes of my consciousness through world events in 1985. I was graduating high school, while Keith was creating jobs in a far-flung African country spotlighted on the word stage for its Apartheid. That summer, the fledgling MTV cable channel incessantly began promoting Bob Geldof's Live Aid concerts. My younger self cynically saw Geldof as an old, washed-up singer from a not so great band who reinvented himself as an activist to feel important again. On the other hand, as a Philadelphian, I was extremely proud that we were hosting the American location and not passed over on the world stage like we normally were for New York or Los Angeles.

Also, that year Stevie Van Zandt put out his collaborative protest war-cry, "Sun City". The incessant chorus of "Ain't Gonna Play Sun City" initially meant absolutely nothing to me. Of course, MTV never explained what or where Sun City was nor the related term Apartheid. Oh, and you couldn't google it to find out for yourself back then. When we finally figured out what the old Baby Boomers were protesting this time, it was not lost on my generation the complete hypocrisy, that the same people telling the rest of the world to boycott South Africa, for human rights violations, were also the very same people who either had or continued to make money from playing Sun City.

My presumption about vehement protesting hasn't changed much over the years. Of course, Shakespeare says it best, "The lady doth protest too much." In my view, whatever people choose to protest is often tied up in some personal projection of their own guilt onto others.

To quote from Flaubert's *Madame Bovary*, "It is better not to touch our idols: the gilt comes off on our hands." Or to quote from my own belief system, it's better not to have any idols, instead look inward and find your own still voice. How ironic while the music industry was trying their best to starve the most vulnerable South Africans to death with their well-meaning but disruptive anti-Apartheid boycotts, Keith had to sneak into the country to create jobs and keep their people alive.

Jolted from my reverie, I blurted out, "But how did you get to South Africa then? It was Apartheid, you weren't allowed to fly there!"

With an upward roll of his eyes, Keith agreed, "Yes, it was awful. We couldn't fly directly from America because of the boycotts. First, I had to fly to London, then I could take a second flight from London to Johannesburg, it took FOR-EVER!"

At this point my heart started to break, no I should say melt. I had been emotionally alone, for so long. And here was this man. No, MAN, who could manage and transgress each and every boundary. Yes, international boundaries, but specifically mine, effortlessly and breathlessly. So much for my impervious bullet-proof veneer. Where had he been? No, where had I been? Because clearly, Keith had been a wild job creator, while I was struggling to pass the CPA exam and navigate my own complicated family life.

*~ Comparing others' timelines to Your own builds Empathy and Understanding ~*

# THE EXCEPTIONAL CAPE COD

## ~ *When we Listen, our Minds Expand* ~

We had finished one cocktail, which was not something I did much of in my busy life. Therefore, I had a narrow list of selections in my memory bank. I had first ordered a Cape Cod. It was something refreshing and simple to ask for, or in today's bar speak a Vodka-Cran. As I looked up over the bar, the large tilted, gilt-framed mirrors, reflected the entire restaurant behind our backs. I decided not to mix drinks, as we ordered another round. What the heck was going on here, a second round? I was so amped up on adrenaline, I didn't even feel the alcohol.

One of the reasons I didn't drink much, is I trusted NO ONE, especially in a work environment. I wanted to remain in control at all times, even back in college. But here I was relaxed with a powerful man and complete stranger, hoping the clocks remained stopped, while I sipped on a cocktail.

This is the moment that I started to believe that one person could have lived in past lives, because I was already familiar with this man's soul. Somewhere deep down where I kept secrets from myself, that place knew my lonely heart had finally come home, even though the rest of me still practiced a healthy dose of denial.

Keith had ordered some appetizers, one that was as exotic to me as cocktail hour, an artichoke dip. It looked like a Bloomin' Onion, but it was a grilled flowering artichoke. You would use your front teeth to scrape off the artichoke meat from the hard-exterior skin, after it was dipped in a ranch like dressing. It was quite beautiful to look at, but also quite a weird process compared to my daily late night snack ritual of a bowl of cereal. As I decided to return to the more familiar French fries, Keith continued the story.

"After we got Mr. Oppenheimer's approval to talk to a competing mine, albeit much smaller, to meet the growing platinum demand driven by technological advances, we started to get down to business. Our first serious meeting to turn our idea into reality was at one of South Africa's largest private game reserves. It was situated in the sprawling savannah adjacent to Kruger National Park. I brought two of my team members, Ian McLean and Bill Lohman. Ian was and still is a genius trader. He could make more money with two phones and a desk then an operating plant on some days. But it was also big-time risk. Terence brought his brother, Kevin the CFO and Ed Haslam the sales director."

"We spent each morning on a game drive viewing wild life such as elephants, lions, rhinos and leopards roaming free. This was how Terence liked to do business, play hard and work hard. It was a way to see people as they really were, how they were going to behave when facing the unexpected. I learned a lot from Terence in this way. One of the things I loved that he did was, if he was reminiscing about a friend, he would call them right on the spot to check in. After the recreational safari, we returned to the luxury camp to discuss the beginnings of what became the most remarkable deal of my career."

I couldn't help getting onto one of my Libertarian (no not liberal, it's the opposite, less bloated bureaucratic government) fiscally conservative rants, "I always love how academic elites act like money just grows on trees planted in a business garden. They really believe that it just happens like a snap of the fingers. That the river will always flow and it is their divinely appointed job to control the perpetual overflowing largesse and take the biggest cut." How come hard work is penalized by those who don't? But I didn't want to distract further from the story, so I let Keith start up again.

"Both teams were comfortable that we both could benefit from the deal. But how to minimize the risks, which could be absolutely devastating to the point of bankruptcy. How to make it that both supplier and buyer, two independent companies couldn't harm the other, when their goals didn't mesh in a particular time period?"

"None of us were sure yet of how to answer that particular question. So, we all went back home and started puzzling on this problem and talking with our business associates some more."


*~ Collaboration leads to Innovation ~*

# SIGNPOSTS

## ~ *Listen to what your tummy tells you* ~

It was at this point, my over stimulated mind needed to break from complicated abstractions. We busied ourselves with our entrees. Since the Palm Beach Grill is actually a Houston's Steak House, we each had a steak with the normal accoutrements.

Over dinner, Keith explained why Houston's had to re-brand itself under a local pseudonym, to earn the right to sell its wares in one of the highly posh United States zip codes, 33480. The powers in charge had decreed that it was not "town serving" to have such a crass chain name as Houston's between its fichus lined streets. Apparently, it was too common to sell food under a brand name. I didn't really get it, since earlier, I had driven down its iconic shopping street, Worth Avenue. It was lined with retail brand names such as Chanel, Tiffany's, Ralph Lauren ad nauseam. What was the difference really between overpriced steak and haute couture? It seemed a bit hypocritical or at minimum splitting a few hairs.

I distracted myself with Keith's impeccable state of dress. Yes, he was dressed casually, but with this flair of subtle sophistication, I had rarely seen on a man. Underneath his navy-blue blazer, he had on this beautiful pink pastel golf-polo shirt, with an embroidered logo on the left chest, instead of the typical screen-printed variation. The material looked like it was made with some outrageous thread count that I had never seen in a Macy's store. His belt, was ringed with tiny embroidered logos as well. Lastly, his loafers were adorned with a beautiful basket weave of leather strands ranging in colors from camel to chocolate, that just made my mouth water.

By this time, we were some of the last in the restaurant, a foreshadowing of the years to come. The hostess had seated us at a table in a quiet corner. I had begun to guzzle down a couple cups of coffee. The long day of travel, wining and dining finally was winning the race with my adrenaline rush. We were toying with dessert options, not wanting this magical summit to end, when we were approached by another man.

It was a golfing friend of Keith's, Bob. As they made light conversation, Bob's curiosity was satisfied with my presence explained. Then Bob stated "Keith I didn't know you were a member of Laurel Valley, Arnold Palmer's golf course. What a great course."

Initially, I viewed this as a form of mind reading, until I realized that golfing men would look at these tiny embroidered sign posts on each other's shirts and belts to see where they each belonged. It was a subtle way of sizing each other up, without having to ask each other a lot of questions. You could choose to engage if you wanted to. How straightforward, it was like a secret handshake that only the members would recognize. Another signpost in a distant land far away from my homeland of Keurig coffee makers and digital timesheets.

Instead of dessert, we decided to continue the night at a local piano bar that I had already heard about in the ladies' room, The Leopard Lounge. We hadn't gotten to the final stories about the mining expansion, and we were clearly getting the signal that it was time for us to leave this gleaming granite and dark mahogany edifice. Soiled tablecloths were flicked off table tops around us in a flurry of motion, like sails on ships going out to sea.

*~ Look for Symbolic Signposts*
*along your Road ~*

# WE WILL TAKE EVERY OUNCE

*~ With Time and Trust,*
*one builds lifetime Partnerships ~*

A magical valet whipped Keith's Lexus SC430, to the front door with as much flair as was possible from its parking space a few yards away. Keith punched a button to bring the hard-top convertible down, which allowed the clear still Florida night to come in all around us. The blonde mahogany wood of the dashboard shone in the silvery moonlight as Keith fiddled with some more buttons to align the correct CD in the auto changer. This was back before Spotify playlists and the invention of digital music. And before Jack Johnson became the global brand he is today, I heard for the very first time the opening bars of "Inaudible Melodies" as if he had written it just for us. Jack began crooning, "Brushfire Fairy Tales, itsy bitsy diamond wells, big fat hurricanes... dust off your thinking caps...slow down everyone your moving too fast...inaudibly free..."

And it was true. There was an inaudible, invisible brushfire raging between us. There were dueling bands in my head now, as if we were flipping between channels, Jack kept getting interrupted by the

Scorpions wailing, "Here I am, rock you like a hurricane."

Almost magnetically, I inched a bit closer to see Keith's profile in the dark. He turned his head, looking dead into my eyes, daring me to kiss him. I completely lost my nerve, and turned my face skyward. I could see the Milky Way much clearer than at home in the big city. Jack began to croon again "when stars were just the holes to heaven".

After finding another alert valet stand, we walked into The Leopard Lounge. There was a piano and singer performing in the bar with little tables recessed among potted palms. Here too was the trademark dark mahogany wood, clubby like Floridian plantations of old. As we settled in at the beautiful long bar, Keith picked up the South African mining tale again.

"I said 'We will take every ounce that you produce,' looking right at Terence in our third and final meeting in the bush. Terence was shocked. He said, 'What? What if we can produce umpteen million ounces of platinum? What are you going to do then?' Terence had every right not to believe us. It was millions of American dollars and about six times more in South African Rand to expand their only mine, buy another and build another. They could put out all this investment into infrastructure, then create more platinum product, and what if we then said no, we didn't want it?"

Keith continued, "We all couldn't bet wrong, it would bankrupt them and possibly their principal investor Tiny Rowland of London fame. If you haven't heard of him in the precious metals world, you will know of his famous store, Harrod's."

"And we had to have a plan if for some reason we didn't sell all the catalytic converters the world needed, or the price went nuts or some other unforeseen disaster. There was another reason why we could do this, we owned our own precious metals trading desk. At this time, we were close to being one of the largest in the world for platinum group metals. The ability to trade metals, gave us the flexibility to sell metal we were not using in industrial products. We had more than one way to make money. Of course, this was key, but this is a different chapter in the story. I will try to stay on point. It won't matter. We'll take it. It will take years for you to get to that point of production, so we can plan for it. We are prepared to sign a contract for it all now."

It was clear that Keith enjoyed telling me these tales of business acumen, almost as much as I loved listening to them. Even that first night, I began a clumsy attempt to assemble a mental catalogue. But it was also sadly clear, that no one close to Keith was listening to this worldly wisdom. Even though we were living in different worlds, we silently recognized that for a long time, we were very alone inside of our own minds.

Continuing Keith rumbled on, "At that point, Bill said, 'Now if we could just find a way for none of us to lose any money.' We were sitting around inside a Bomba, which is a wooden fenced enclosure with a bonfire in the middle. It was the safest way to have an outdoor campfire in the middle of the African bush, where predatory animals roamed freely. We chewed on Biltong, which is dried meat, and sipped scotch by the fire. We were all mulling over pricing methods that would be fair to each party, so neither party could harm the other."

"Then an idea came to me to solve the problem for Terence's South African team. I said, 'what if Lonrho had the ability in the contract to trigger an option NOT to mine twice a year, if they thought they were going to lose money due to a drop in platinum prices? On January first and July first, they could come back and tell us, we aren't mining for the next six months. Then if they had to, they could trigger it again every six months. They had to deal with things like government regulations and striking miners, that we couldn't control nor predict. They needed an option that they wouldn't be required to mine at a loss. This was while all the craziness of apartheid was happening too."

I fingered the base of the beautiful bronze sculpture of a heron (or was it an egret?), placed on the bar. Well, I knew I could rule out the urban pigeon! While contemplating the bird's possible genetics, I asked, "How many times did the Africans ever have to trigger the NO-GO option?"

I was surprised when Keith made a zero with his thumb and index finger.

Keith said, "Having the freedom to opt out was the key. It gave them autonomy and removed a big stumbling block of the fearful unknown."

"Who came up with the idea for the No-Lose Clause for your side?"

"Well when I was talking about the idea to help Lonrho, I noticed Ian McLean was not really mentally engaged and was working on a problem in his own head. I asked him if he had come up with anything. His trading mind had. Our issue was we couldn't predict the price of the platinum group metals into eternity, so how do you control the price?"

"Ian suggested the following option. On the first of each month, we could look backwards for thirty days and pick the average price for that month. Alternatively, we could set the price on the first of each month based on the future month's average price."

I asked, "But if it is the unknown future price, how do you predict that?"

"This was where Ian's trading genius found a flexible solution. We would hedge one thirtieth of the future price each day. That way, we wouldn't lose if the price started increasing. We would make the money back on the hedge we put into place, a hedge effectively being a little insurance policy."

"Wow! Now that makes my head hurt, just thinking about it! How many times did you use past or future month's pricing?" I was curious.

"More times than not, we used the past price, because generally the price of platinum was going upwards on the graph. This was due to the new industrial uses we discovered for platinum, so the past month's price was usually cheaper. Maybe only once or twice we used the future price."

*~ Remove the Fear of losing*
*and a Partnership becomes Powerful ~*

# CALCULATING EUPHORIA

*~ When its Mutually Beneficial
it becomes Intoxicating ~*

As the night was coming to a close, Keith wrapped up the story:

"It was this meeting in Mala Mala, where we committed the deal to two pieces of paper, front and back. We actually signed it each of us. It was at this point that Ed Haslam, Terence's sales guy, who lived in Brussels, started punching numbers into his calculator. Ed was trying to figure the number of ounces mined over the next three to five years multiplied by what he thought the price could be, in South African Rand. At the time, six Rand were equal to one dollar. The number was so big, the calculator couldn't hold it all, therefore we couldn't tell what the revenue and profits were in Rand. So, Ed threw the calculator against the wall and it broke into a bunch of pieces. 'Well, the one thing we do know is it's gonna be a whole lot of f*$king money!' crowed Ed. We all started laughing and knew that we had the potential to do something really great together."

*~ Whoever loses the Least Wins ~*

# LAUNCHED: FROM IDEA TO PAPER

### ~ *Don't let the paper pushers override Future Benefits* ~

"The next step in the process was to turn the two little pieces of paper and turn it into a proper agreement.  So, each side gave a copy of our signed document to our lawyers.  We told them, we didn't want it to be more than ten pages, in an effort to keep the lawyering from messing up our deal.  Often lawyers feel like the way to make their jobs relevant they gotta line the agreement with a whole bunch of little gotchas.  Often this can sour a great deal, when the lawyers get involved.  In this case, neither side could control the lawyers totally on this matter. We ended up with twelve pages of an agreement and about a twenty-four page addendum.  They wanted to iron out details such as pricing mechanisms, what day it occurred, what time of day, what average price, are we talking about New York Time or London Time, the NYMEX stock price or whatever. That took about two months to turn it into a deal that we could all agree with."

Funnily, it as at this point that Keith was fired up enough in his recall of various run-ins with paper pushers, that he forgot he was talking to one of them, me.

"It was always the tax people, that drove me nuts. We'd have all the details of a deal worked out, and it would always be the tax guy changing his answer at the last minute that could blow it up. Ahhh would ending up saying, if you move again, I'm gonna shoot you between the eyes!"

Bursting out laughing, I replied, "Well as a tax person myself, I would say this: Facts Drive Tax! And you people would never give us the full story. You would leave out some facts that you didn't realize were relevant, which of course created an entirely different tax answer! That's why I ask so many questions, because invariably it draws out some fact that is a game changer."

At that point, Keith refocused his eyes on my face, and cracked a smile. "But isn't that what I pay them a boatload of money for? There is nothing more than violated expectations, that drives me mad! What was I saying? Now, we were finally at the point to formally present it to our respective boards. Each side had to keep our bosses informed with progress reports along the way. It was time to get their approvals to move forward."

"I had received my boss' verbal ok to present it to our board and recommend it.  I told Terence, that our side had progressed.  It was time for Terence to present our deal to his boss and major investor, Tiny Rowland."


*~Details Matter.*

*Must Solve first to Win required Approvals ~*

# HARROD'S OF LONDON

## ~ *Violated Expectations*
## *are hard to Overcome* ~

"Tiny was the CEO of Lonrho PLC in London which owned Lonrho SA of South Africa, Terence's mining company. The nickname most have been an irony, because Tiny was a very large man."

"This is really a side story with a bit of color. Tiny Rowland was having a difficult time with the British Government. They were angry about things that he had said in the papers, because he didn't have a lot of respect for the governance people nor the crown of England. Since he owned his own paper, he could voice his opinions pretty easily. But this wasn't America, they have different rules over there about free speech which is a lot more limiting. Al Fayed was another guy in town that owned his own newspaper. They were friendly competitors, Fayed chose to take up the government's position in the papers opposing Tiny's expressed views. In response to Tiny's position, the British government threatened to take Harrod's Department Store away from him as a punishment for blackening the Crown's name or something like that. So Tiny called up Fayed, because even though they were competitors they were also peers that respected each other. Tiny asked if he could "park" his Harrod's shares with Fayed in his name and title to protect it from confiscation by the crown."

I had to interrupt for a moment, "I didn't realize you could do that in England, because that isn't something so easily done in America. It could be considered a trigger of IRS compensation rules. Also, I'm not a lawyer, but I don't think you can really park shares like that without creating a whole bunch of titling issues in the United States," which was about all the ammunition I had on that topic.

With a quick nod of his head Keith rambled on, "Yeah, I agree they got a lot of other weird rules over there. But at the end of the day when the firestorm was over, Fayed refused to honor the agreement. And he kept the shares of Harrods never to be returned, which drove Tiny nuts!"

"Wait a minute, is this the same Fayed? Was this Dodi Fayed's Dad? The Dodi Fayed that was engaged and killed in Paris with Princess Diana?" I conjectured.

With another small smile, "Yes the very same one."

I murmured, "Things do come back around in strange ways sometimes, don't they?"

With that we both took a sip of our after dinner drinks and contemplated the strange scales of justice.

The duo was singing Eric Clapton's mournful, "Would you know my name, if I saw you in heaven." It is the heart breaking song about the loss of Eric's young son who fell to his death from a Pre-World War II building's open window in downtown Manhattan. How apropos based on the story of another father's tragic loss of his son on the world stage, in a tunnel with perhaps the world's most famous woman.

Thank God we didn't know at that time, how a similar twist of fate would take a loved one too young and too early from our future selves. There are small mercies living in the present with the future carefully wrapped in a foggy haze.

Keith picked up the thread again, "Terence sent the finished deal documents to Mr. Rowland and discussed it with him personally. But they were big numbers, big enough to shake up Lonrho of London, if things went sideways. Therefore, Tiny asked for a personal meeting with me, before he endorsed the transaction. After his personal approval, he planned to present it to HIS board of directors for final sign off. If it was a go, it entailed his board making an investment numbering in the billions of South African Rand to expand their platinum mines."

"Tiny said he wanted 'to see the whites of my eyes' before doing this big-time deal. So, I flew to London where Terence and I went together to meet Tiny alone for about an hour and twenty minutes at his headquarters in London. I left, then Terence called me and told me that the interview had gone really well. Tiny was now prepared to support it at his board meeting. About a month later I presented the agreement to my Board at Engelhard. Oppenheimer had three guys on our board, since they were our major shareholders, and were also platinum supply competitors. Hippo was his CFO, which I'm forgetting his real name right now, but everyone called him Hippo. You can imagine how he earned his moniker. Anyway, the deal was approved and set for signatures from our side. Our board formally approved it as a whole. Since Oppenheimer was also our supplier of platinum, they needed to officially endorse that they approved our buying our raw material elsewhere, when they couldn't meet all of our needs."

"Terence and I agreed to meet when both sides were done with their review and approvals. Lonrho's board meeting was about a month after ours, then Terence and I planned to meet up in Paris three or four days afterwards. We were both confident it would be a completed deal, and so we booked a real fancy restaurant in Paris, Le Taillevent. It has the highest rating possible, a Michelin three star. It was known to have over half a million bottles of wine in its cellars, but one hundred percent of it is Bordeaux wine. Some of it even survived Nazi occupation during World War II somehow."

"It was the original six of us that had started it all in the African Bush: Bill Lohman and Ian McLean, and myself from our side. Terence, his brother Kevin and Ed Haslam from South Africa's side. Those three guys were in London the prior day. Terence took three of our signed originals contracts to his board meeting. By noon the next day, Terence and his team arrived in Paris for our celebratory dinner reservation. Terence strolled in and handed me two signed copies. Finally, we were official! Due to the time differences, I could still call my CEO back in New Jersey and deliver the great news in real time!"

"We now had a future rock-solid platinum supplier to meet the world's newly required industrial use. Markets hate uncertainty, that's when stock prices plummet. Our deal bought us a lot of stability."

Giggling, I started humming "Sahhhhh-liddddd, Solid as a rock!" under my breath. It was that 1984 hit by husband and wife team Ashford & Simpson, where she starts out acapella and Ashford joins in.

*~ Markets hate uncertainty,*
*clear Communication brings Stability ~*

# FROM PAPER TO ROCK SOLID

### ~ *Ideas come in a Flash,* *Implementation is hard Work* ~

"Our deal was rock solid. It was time for Terence's team to start the really complex process of building out mines, hiring thousands of new people, training them in new skills, developing their physical stamina to be able to work underground in the heat. A myriad of stuff had to be done."

Keith paused and reflected further:

"After the deal was signed and approved by company boards, Lonrho really began to focus on what they could do with that deal. How do we actually expand? They made two primary decisions very quickly. Number one was to expand the mining effort at the existing Western Platinum Mine. Two, build a completely new one called Eastern Platinum about four or five miles away from Western. The original mine was fully built out above the ground. It had conveyor belt systems to move the mined ore to the first stage of concentration. This stage was located at the mine where the platinum group metals were taken from the ore. The resulting end product of precious metals is only a few ounces per ton of ore. This first tier of the concentrator process gets the amalgamated precious metals to about sixty to seventy percent purity. The end result is five distinct platinum group metals each refined to a .9999 purity. But the final finesse took place at their primary refinery located about seventy- five miles away just outside of Johannesburg."

I interjected, "That makes economical sense. If you have to pay to move product around, you would want to minimize as much of the bulky waste as possible. Its mind boggling how tiny the end product is after the extraction process from the ton of ore. On its face, it doesn't seem possible that it could still be a profitable endeavor, does it? When you say platinum group metals, what are the other ones besides platinum then?"

"Well there are actually six I think." With that Keith unfurled his burly fingers again, with their square tips and neatly clipped fingernails.

"Platinum, palladium, iridium, rhodium, ruthenium and osmium make six. They are refined to 99.9% pure, then the platinum is made into bars that are one to two kilos each. From there the metal was shipped by air to their customers. The precious cargo was highly guarded on its travels all the way into the hands of its buyers. Whether it be on the roads, or on the airplane until it reached a customer's secure location in whatever country they were located in. For us at Engelhard, Brinks Armored Car Service would pick up our product in New York City."

"Upon delivery, we stored the metal in our own vaults until it was to put to use or sold. We used about 95% of the metal we purchased and sold about 5% on the market. But because platinum can be bought and sold on paper only, similar to buying stocks and bonds, such as the NYMEX, which is called a terminal exchange."

I interjected, "Oh, platinum is like gold and silver? Why not the other metals too? Were they not used as widely?" I was thinking of the endless commercials encouraging us to buy paper certificates in gold and silver, because the world was going to end soon.

Keith replied, "Yes, platinum and palladium didn't have to be a physical transaction. But interestingly enough that wasn't true about the other four metals. I think it was probably a combination of a few things including demand. But I think metal producers would get together and decide as a group they weren't going to list it on an exchange, to maintain more price control."

"Sometime in 1987 I think; the new mine was started. It took Terence's company about one and a half years to completely build it out. This meant sinking the mine shaft and creating massive silos to hold ore. Rather than build a second concentration plant the ore was shipped by truck to Western Platinum's processing plant. This doubled the capacity of the processing plant, which meant the company was more efficient. It only required increasing the size of the original plant some, because all of the chemicals, electronics, boilers were already there."

"So, this is definitely an example for your value principle, 'Get more of the good stuff'," I commented.

With a brief nod of his head, Keith continued to roll, "Exactly! Once, Lonrho South Africa realized just how great this deal was (We will buy everything that you produce) they were off to the races. They wanted to have immediate additional capacity and not want to wait another two years to build yet another mine. So, they approached a smaller mining company and bought Karee Mine. After completing their research, they figured they could go from producing sixty thousand ounces of platinum per year to three-hundred and fifty or even five hundred thousand per year without as much intense investment. Thereby by 1988, Terence's team expanded the existing WPL, outright built EPL and acquired Karee. From a standing start, their platinum production had gone from approximately one hundred and twenty thousand ounces per year to over five hundred ounces in a few years. Today, after Terence and I are long gone, those same mines are producing about one million four hundred thousand ounces per year. This HUGE amount of risk-taking to build out mines for future use is WHY we needed an airtight deal to ensure no one was a loser."

More quietly in an almost reverent tone, Keith murmured, "I have three commissioned paintings hanging in my home today of these mines. Every day, they remind me of what we achieved in that amazing venture."

*~ Make good Assumptions*
*until Proven Wrong ~*

# WHAT MAKES PEOPLE TICK

*~ Ask Questions before Acting*
*on what you Presume ~*

"When Terence and his team built the entirely new Eastern Platinum, they needed to consider housing needs for the thousands of new employees. Think of the mining towns in our own Wild West. That is what they were up against. To accommodate the miners, they built an entire town from the ground up. The government gave them approval to build this beautiful all brick facility, sporting fields, a bar, stores and housing."

"Terence wanted everything to be top of the line and considerate of both single miners and married men that already had families, therefore they were planning to supply two kinds of housing. The first offering was for the single miners with very modern dorm spaces. But he wanted to provide miners with family a more stable option. He would build individual brick homes for any miner and his family. They could choose home ownership and obtain a mortgage or rent it. Each house was solid brick, with three to four bedrooms, a modern kitchen and appliances, turnkey housing in effect."

Impressed myself, I interjected, "Wow, that was really far sighted thinking! He was trying to do things for the long term, wasn't he?"

Keith continued, "But Terence was shocked after talking with the miners' lead representatives. Very few miners wanted to buy the houses, they mostly preferred the dorms, with a few exceptions. Terence wanted to understand why, so he went and talked to the Head Miner of the mostly black South Africans. They had two main reasons for rejecting the home ownership model, that were based on their own cultural mores."

"First, the land was not owned by their tribe, the Khoisan, it was Zulu land. Regardless of the legal title on paper, the land was not for sale out of respect to the Zulus. Two, the miners actually liked to be on location away from their wives for four to six months out of a year!"

Laughing along with Keith, I had to add my two cents, "As I was saying, if one asks a lot of questions, it leads to discovering important new facts!"

*~ Do you want to make a Decision
with more or less Data? ~*

# TAKE TIME TO CELEBRATE SUCCESS

### ~ *Reflect, Embrace roles, and Extend Success* ~

"We had a big celebration when Terence and his company, Lonrho opened the brand new mine, EPL. Ian, Bill, myself and all our wives flew over from the United States. South Africa's Minister of Mineral Resources and several others, like our Minister of the Interior, but I forget what their country's title was. Then technical people from the world's Platinum Associates, a bunch a people from Lonrho in London came down too. Don't think this exists anymore, but there was an area inside of South Africa that was considered independent. It was pronounced Bow-pit-so-wanna, don't know how to spell it though! Anyway, their president came too. This is where I presented Lonrho with the painting I commissioned called "Partners" that hangs in EPL's board room today. I was quite taken aback when they presented me with the first ounce of platinum that was mined out of EPL the brand new mine."

"When you look at a world map, it isn't clear how large South Africa really is, since the African continent is so big itself. Then add in the distortions of flattening out a globe into two dimensions, its physical dimension doesn't remain true, but it's almost as large in scale as the United States."

"That is shocking!" I interrupted. "I did start this awesome book by John Reader, *Africa: Biography of a Continent*, which I need to finish. But he talks about the huge scale of Africa a bit. I remember he had some map in there where a huge number of countries from around the world included as an overlay of the whole African continent, and it basically swallows us all whole. How Africa is the keystone continent that doesn't move, while all the rest of us drift away and back towards it as the massive lynchpin, over millions of years."

Nodding in agreement, Keith continued, "Yeah, if you flew there you would see for yourself, you can fly South over the continent all day long. So back to South Africa, it's so large that it is not easy to get around so easily. It's not like here in America where Eisenhower took money out of our Defense budget to build the infrastructure of our highway system that we all still use today. I think Ike called it a national emergency. It was the Cold War Era and emotions ran high about nuclear mutual destruction. The highways would allow military and citizens to move quickly about the country to escape death by nuclear fallout and radiation poisoning."

"So South Africa is similar in size to us, but their highway systems aren't near the quantity or quality of our roads, especially up in mining country. One of the efficient tricks the mines used was to build dual-purpose roads. One section was quite long and really well built, so it could double as a landing strip for airplanes. Out of necessity, companies were required to use small planes to move about the Eastern Transvaal, where the platinum mines were located. Pragmatic Terence, relied on a small plane to move about the country more efficiently. He got interested enough that he had his pilot teach him how to fly, because he enjoyed it so much."

"I really loved working with the Wilkinson brothers, they were full of life and fun. Terence's older brother was Kevin, whom played an important role as the finance director. It was an interesting family dynamic that worked for them. Terence was the younger brother, but was Kevin's boss. They worked well together. Terence was the practical joker. One time I was in the car with Ed and the two brothers. Ed was in the back seat giving Terence a bunch of lip, so Terence pushed in the cigarette lighter to heat it up, then threw it in the back seat to get back at Ed. Of course, Ed was screaming and carrying on and Terence was laughing his A$$ off."

After laughing over that visual image, I paused because I recognized a pattern, so I added, "Sounds like one of my client stereotypes, The Entrepreneur Duo, with a front man and back room guy. Kevin would be the back room man running the numbers.

While Terence is the front sales guy flying around the country building relationships."

Keith shared, "Yes, Kevin had to make a lot of decisions around currencies and conversions. In essence he was their Treasury function. When they sold us platinum, we of course paid them in U.S. Dollars, our currency. They had to turn them into South African currency, the Rand. Their country's laws and regulations required them to pay their employees in Rand."

Suddenly an image of Danny Glover and Mel Gibson stranded on a container ship flashed into my head. They were flushing out the evil South African villains caught transporting massive amounts of South African gold coins. I always loved to parrot the final line falling from the bad guy's lips 'Diplomatic Immunity!' as Danny Glover shoots him between the eyes, or was it Mel?

As images of gold coins with little antelope on them were dancing before my eyes, I blurted out, "Da ya mean the Krueger Rand?"

"No that was the gold coin. The Rand is their paper dollar, that today ranges around six Rand to One U.S. dollar. Anyway, as one can imagine, currency fluctuations could really help or harm their company. They had the world's platinum price fixed every day in U.S. Dollars, just like oil is today. They had the cost of getting the platinum out of the ground. Then they were obligated to turn our payments into Rand to pay all of their overhead. Kevin had a lot of weight riding on his shoulders, as he had the Treasury Function for the whole South African thang. Besides the platinum, Lonrho had a bunch of other interests. A big one was coal. They had been mining coal for so long they exported coal around the world, since they were so efficient at it. As a Treasurer, you are responsible for banking, borrowing, currency exchanges, trading, so Kevin had a lot of responsibilities too."

"Terence was like many CEOs, you have to make countless tough decisions that affect a legion of people. Everyone that comes to your office, comes with their own agenda or multiple agendas. You don't necessarily know what they are, so you get quite cagey in expressing your inner thoughts, because you don't trust how others may use that information. I know, because I had the same issues in my life. As I said before, violated expectations are the cause of many conflicts. Often, it was easier to keep one's views close to the vest. We got this about each other, but despite all of that, or maybe because of it, Terence was one of my friends that I admired the most."

"These South Africans formed a really tight knit group, in some ways they were up against a lot of people. Terence, Kevin, Peter, Ian, Max, Barry and Ed. You really become foxhole companions, in something this big. I was honored that they let me be

a part of their celebration and relaxation in the Bush.
It meant a lot to me."

*~ Remember to Celebrate Success,*
*especially with those Closest to You ~*

# NOW SARAH

## ~ *Irreverence sometimes is a Celebration of Survival* ~

The bar was winding down for the evening, so I ordered some hot tea to warm up, since between ice cubes and frigid Floridian air conditioning, I was getting a bit too chilly. We were still talking about South Africa. Keith was telling more of Terence's shenanigans, such as throwing elephant dung into the top of an open air shower while out in the bush, and other moments of levity, depending on if you were on the giving or receiving end. He wrapped up this segment with a kicker of a story.

"On one of my negotiation trips, we were at Mala Mala. This was somewhere in the middle of our discussions. A good friend of Terence's showed up, named Anton Rupert. Anton was the CEO and principal investor in the Rembrandt Group, a very wealthy guy. One day, Terence came into lunch and said Anton called and asked if he and a lady friend could join us at Mala Mala, for the rest of the day. They would fly in the afternoon from Johannesburg and go on the evening and morning animal drives with us. Anton was about seventy at the time. He showed up with this drop dead beautiful twenty something year old woman, Sarah. We had tea at four and climbed into the open vehicles around five pm. Terence and I were with Anton and his date Sarah in the one vehicle. Anton asked the ranger if he could please try to spot a leopard today, because Sarah has never seen one. It's not so easy to see everything, its not like the zoo. These people were all South Africans, whom had lived their whole lives there. They hadn't necessarily seen the Big Five or all of the Magnificent Seven. The Five includes Lion, Rhino, Cape Buffalo, Leopard, and Elephant. The Cheetah and African Wild Hunting Dog make it seven. So, Sarah had still not seen a leopard. We were all on the hunt! We were driving along, and we would stop and see other animals that he had spotted. These could range from predator to prey. Over the course of time the wild animals had adapted to the tracking vehicles. They knew they were not vehicles that would harm them, so the animals just ignored the trucks as not a predator or prey, just neutral."

"Like Switzerland," I joked.

Smiling Keith went on, "But the ranger was checking for leopard's spores, otherwise known as animal tracks. It got dark. From the vehicle, the ranger was tracing a line of light with his flashlight. Finally, he found something. He opened the door and kept looking down as we drove along. Finally, we got into a river bed that was dried out and the bottom was mostly sand. We drove about one quarter mile down the dried-out river bed. Stopping the vehicle, the guy turned it off. Then he took a light and shined it up into the tree above us saying quietly, 'Now if I got it right, she would be right up there'. And there she was in all of her glory chewing on her latest kill of Impala!"

"Our small group sat spellbound looking up into the dark branches, where the ranger's flashlight lit an eerie halo around the Leopard's head and massive jaws working through the fleshy throat of her kill. I rubbed my own neck a bit, realizing how easy it would be for a leopard to snap a human's neck like a match stick. It was then we heard Anton's clear tenor express his dry take on this predatory scene, 'Now, Sarah, there's some serious pussy'!"

"With that we all howled, breaking the unspoken stream of morbid thoughts. The ranger got a little nervous because our raucous fray was getting the leopard a little annoyed, so we slowly backed our open vehicle away from her leafy perch. To memorialize this amazing evening, I later framed a photograph that I took of a leopard on that trip. One of my favorites that I've ever taken, and sent it as a gift to each member of our safari party, with the moniker, 'serious pu$$y" on the back of each one."

~ *Revel in each Moment,*
*for this is All we Own* ~

# HEART IN HAND

## ~ *Carpe Diem: Seize the Day* ~

It was then that I noticed Keith's gold college signet ring, on his square, strong fingers. I wondered where he had gone to school. I expected that it was some unattainable Ivy League Business School, based on his tales of high finance. But yet again, this Renaissance Man's response smashed my stereotype. Right now, I just kept thinking about his hands, and how strongly they could emphasize his point...and how they might feel. Quickly, I shook my head to clear my thoughts. When I could trust myself to speak sanely, I asked, which Ivy League school did he attend.

In a booming voice, "Hell no! I came from a little, pee wee town in the back woods of South Carolina. I went to the Una-verse-uh-teee of South Carrow-Line-Ahh."

It wasn't a hard, hard Southern Drawl, but the consonants were a lot softer than what I heard every day on the streets of Philadelphia (to quote Bruce Springsteen).

"I could have gotten my MBA at Harvard, when they gave me a scholarship, but I knew I had some of the greatest professors in the world right where I was. I was also engaged at the time to Susan, a really nice Southern gal. Not only did I get a full ride at South Carolina's School of Business, I was paid a stipend for living expenses if I stayed on. After the training, I got from my Economics professors I knew I could go toe to toe with any Ivy Leaguer from the Northeast."

As Keith spoke, he turned around to shoo away an encroaching barfly. She was trying to push us down the bar so she could squeeze into the first row. I was suddenly mesmerized by his broad, thick shoulders that appeared in my line of vision. Wow, I could now picture his swimmer's back plowing through the water in that record setting breaststroke, that Keith had already described. Wait, he was talking to me again, I had to put away these emotional distractions and focus on listening.

*~ Embrace what makes You Different ~*

# MINISTER OF MY INTERIOR

*~ Be gentle when another let's you walk*
*their Sacred Ground ~*

After a few moments of suspended silence, Keith reflected further:

"I've had an amazing life. I know a lot of people wouldn't believe half the stuff that I've done and that has happened to me. Sometimes it doesn't even seem to me that they all can be true, even to me and I'm the one that lived it!"

I believe I can recognize the difference between the ring of truth and the hollow sound of exaggeration to garner personal attention, more often than not. And this night was full of vim and vigor for sure. But clearly it was the downright truth, because each vignette was told with such granular detail, filled with facts that could easily be verified, with the resounding vibration that only truth can hold. Over the years to come, I got to see some of these marvels with my own eyes, when Keith took me to view the actual mining endeavors, that were birthed from ideas discussed around a campfire in the African Bush. Who knew?

But this night had a confessional type feel to it. No one had been listening to this full-blooded man for a long time. He had been boring through life on one speed wide open, fast and furious. Too busy to slow down. But also, it became clear as he shared each story, it had been a long, lonely road to the top of his mountain. He had climbed obstacles that were probably insurmountable for most others, and as he reached his personal finish line, he was utterly alone.

As if reading my mind, Keith suddenly said, "If I had to pick one word, just one, to describe you, do you know what it would be?"

Jolted from my reverie with the uncomfortable knowledge that Keith had been walking around in the hallways of my brain, I attempted a smile and said, "I've no idea, what?"

And he replied with just one word, "Empathy."

That simply, Keith's hands were holding my heart. It was as if he held the missing key to my secret diary, turning me into an open book, while his burly hands were turning each lucent page of me.

In those first few hours together, he saw ME. Not only did he see how my clock ticked, he had the verve to say exactly what it was that he saw. I had spent years, building a veneer to keep all people on the other side of my fence. I had a lot of practice. I liked to understand others, but didn't necessarily want it to be mutual, based on my own failed experiences with vulnerability, especially in the love department.

But Keith had nailed my hide to the barnyard door, to use another one of his Southern expressions. Not only did I feel for others, often I actually felt others' pain when I was in their presence. In a movie, often I averted my eyes from torture and prison scenes, because I physically held the pain in the pit of my stomach for hours after, and the images never left my mind.

Don't know why, but the ancient expression about make sure you walk in another's shoes before you judge them, is me to a tee. But besides my Pop, no one in my life had ever called me out on it. As a minister, my father spent hours at people's bedsides, when they were sick and dying. He would administer prayers, communion and most importantly love and compassion. An adept at reading people himself, my Pop saw my empathetic soul.

But in this blinding flash of one evening, how did Keith know me? Not only did he see me, he had the B*lls to say it. I would name him the Minister of my Interior in a heartbeat, or as Maya Angelou had penned, he "laid my soul in strips". After this breathless foray into my interior previously uncharted territory, Keith asked with some curiosity, "What would you call me?"

And with that a slideshow began in the front of my vision. I was silently following Keith's broad back. We were dressed in vests of dark animal fur from some ancient place in time. Wending our way through a deciduous thicket of forest, I pivoted silently, off his right shoulder, with my bow and arrow drawn ready to fire.

Without hesitation, I blurted out, "Braveheart! You are the bravest man I know, and you have the heart of a giant."

It was the first time, I got Keith to blink, with surprise. It was quid pro quo. With that question, we started the slow, languorous process of discovering the infinite layers of another soul wrapped in a human skin.

*~ Practice Empathy which requires*
*a Brave Heart ~*

# MANDELA'S LONG WALK
# TO FREEDOM

*~ When you want to know Everything,*
*you are a Game Changer ~*

As we sat on our stools, hunched over the bar, doodling analogies on napkins, the musicians attempted George Michael's ripsnorter song, "Freedom". It didn't sound close to the swashbuckling MTV version with the chorus belted out at gut level, but it was recognizable. Perhaps the musical tribute triggered Keith to confess his interface with Mandela.

"On one of my work trips, I was in South Africa on the day that Nelson Mandela was released from prison. I remember the newspaper headline was really simple, 'HE'S FREE', the font size was such that it took up the entire newspaper page above the fold. He was a quiet force that changed the country for the better. The fear is there is no leader with the soul force to follow and keep the flame burning."

I had to chime in on that point, "I totally believe that model too. When there is a strong charismatic leader, it becomes almost impossible to follow, no matter how great you are. People can't help but to compare the successor to the last guy. I call it the Old Man Syndrome, you hear it all the time, 'who do you think you are your old man? Well you're not!' I see it all the time with my family business clients. Generally, somehow if the business stays in the family, the torch seems to pass more easily from grandfather to grandson, not so much to the son. Occasionally, it appears to be better when it is father to daughter, somehow that seems to work better. We have to wait for the future until I have actual stats on grandmothers being the business matriarch," I said with a sardonic grin.

Keith agreed, chiming in with, "My Mother was a strong woman. Sarah Belle raised me by herself. I could have seen her running a business, if she had the chance. She was a proud college graduate, who wasn't going to put up with any of my own father's nonsense. When I was a toddler, she divorced my Dad. Now mind you this was the South during World War II, this was just not done. She went out and got a job right away, she raised me all by herself. She was tough!"

This was the first time Sarah Belle's ghost entered the room. But she was never far away, over the years we have conjured her up when needed. Today, I've no doubt that much of Keith's career successes were linked to this woman of courage.

"Besides my Mother, Nelson Mandela, was one of the most inspiring people I've ever had the privilege to meet. I got to speak with him alone for about a half hour. What a great man."

"Well that's amazing. I am curious what that conversation was like! I've seen a few random photo-op Mandela pictures, when wandering the halls of the corporate executives at Delta. But upon further inspection it became clear these were staged event photos, 'thank you for your donation' type photos," I interjected.

Keith continued, "It was in 1989, on one of the last trips I made to South Africa that I had the opportunity to meet 'Madiba', that was his personal nickname. Over my career at Engelhard, I believe I counted up about thirty-eight trips to that beautiful country. This meeting happened after Mandela was released from prison on Robben Island and before he was elected the first President of South Africa."

"Whaddya mean first?" I asked curiously.

"Well before Mandela it had always been prime minister. But when they formed a new constitution, with the one man one vote, they did away with the British titles as far as I can recall. The time I'm referencing was this. Mandela was invited to speak to the South African parliament when it started its next session in Cape Town. The country's history was divided for a long time. The Boer Wars reflecting the political divide between the Dutch and the British. As a throwback to that division, South Africa tried to placate both nationalities by dividing its Congress into two geographical locations. For six months of the year, they met in Praetoria for the Dutch. For the remainder of the year, Congress was in session in Cape Town to appease the British. To affect this cumbersome transition, important people took the luxurious Blue Train between the two cities, which was a long one or two day train ride. This was probably equal to a train ride between Phoenix and Miami."

"As this was the 1980's, this required an enormous administrative effort including several rail cars full of the government's paper records in cargo cars, complicated. But the famous Blue Train was re-known for its formal luxurious setting, top shelf. Shortly after Mandela's release from prison, he was invited to board the Blue Train along with numerous important political and industrial national figures. It was a nod to Mandela, that he could now travel in honor for his first public address to the Congress while it resided in Cape Town. People were assigned sleeping cabins, due to the length of the trip. It was quite an event, black tie dining car, all the bells and whistles."

"This was before Mandela negotiated with President de Klerk the 'one man one vote'. Mandela asked important figures from various walks of life to join him, so he could gather as much diverse information as possible to help inform his future decisions and recommendations, for ALL of his fellow countrymen."

"I may have been invited to meet Mandela, because my South African Platinum Association compatriots referred me for the opportunity. I don't really know to be perfectly frank. Based on my view of Mandela, I wouldn't be surprised if he asked to speak to American businessmen working inside his country, so he could expand his own world view."

"Like many others, the work I did with Terence's company was part of the country's growing accretion of wealth, as together we had increased the overall supply of South African platinum to meet the world's demand. I was honored to accept this iconic invitation, and witness these first steps of a brave new world."

"Mr. Mandela was an incredibly peaceful person, which was so easily seen in his eyes. He was respectful and seemed to be a truly caring person for people. Yet he had a back of steel when it come to what his political objectives were for Black South Africans and the members of his own political party, the African National Congress (ANC). He was very soft spoken. The only time I ever saw his demeanor change completely, from this peaceful look was on TV once. He was on some news hook up and was responding to a question about whether his party and other Black South Africans would be willing to literally go to war to fight for their rightful place. Sternly, he affirmed that that was absolutely true. They would fight, if they couldn't win through a peaceful negotiation. He was a different man in that moment."

"I went along to Mandela's passenger lounge car, where he received a continuous stream of visitors, talking to several people at a time, that kinda thing. When it was my turn to be introduced to the great man, we talked about all sorts of things, such as how he planned to run the country after he became the president. He was quite reticent to state that that was definitely going to happen. Yet he was realistic that it was likely."

"All in all, I ended up being alone with Mandela for about forty-five minutes. Mr. Mandela had the attitude of 'Tell me everything you know'."

Inwardly, I couldn't help but smile, because this level of curiosity I could relate to myself. It was how I could sit here riveted to my chair and listen to Keith spin one story after another. Particularly, because I didn't know any of this material from my own experiences. It was as if vistas were flinging open their shutters for me to peer through the annals of time.

Keith said, "Quickly he noted that I was an American, and he wanted to know from me a lot about the United States. He wanted to know who were some of the people in the world that I thought were top-shelf outstanding people. He asked for me to explain the workings of the complex relationships between Engelhard, Lonrho and Anglo American. His curious mind was interested in the details of how these complicated interactions could actually work. We got into the weeds of how many of Engelhard's board members were also Anglo American's board members. How many employees and locations did we have? What kinds of things did we do other than Precious Metals?"

"He was really interested in the concept of fluid cracking catalysts. I roughed out how a cracking tower's physics worked to change a molecule of oil as it fell toward the earth. First the chemical reaction on the oil molecule created naphtha, then gas, then kerosene, fuel oils number one and number two next, and lastly asphalt. It was mostly me answering those kinds of questions for him."

"But I tried to ask questions about morality such as could he get to the point to forgive the white South Africans and serve as President to all races. He had obviously thought about that a lot, so he had the answers at the tip of his tongue what his views were. He seemed to be a very devout, religious godly fellow. He expressed concern about his then wife, Winnie and some of the things that she had done. It was just coming out that while he was in prison, Winnie had hired assassin gangs to remove some of their opposition. Mandela was emphatic on that point, 'We can't have that or it will throw the country into absolute chaos'. His worldly curiosity or tell-me-all attitude led to this wide-ranging discussion. He led us into the developed field of business ethics and the application of values to the established American business world. How did we keep those values? We talked about different industry's business ethical standards and how they developed. He wanted to know practically how we did it in America. An old country developing a new constitution could easily be a vacuum-like black hole where all the well-meaning activism was sucked down the drain if the infrastructure was not there."

I thought of my career in Public Accounting and all of the ethical standards we were required to live and report by ourselves and apply to our clients via such regulatory bodies as the FASB and the SEC. When you are down in the trenches, grumbling about cumbersome application of regulations, it is easy to forget about what the world would look like without fair application of playing rules.

"At Engelhard we had an internal ethics policy and handbook and training. Yet as Americans, we had already experienced enough industrial cheating that we had history to depend on. America had already developed the Foreign Corrupt Practices Act. It was pretty established, so it had a lot of teeth in it already. As a company and its officers, you can get into real trouble with that thing. You have to be pretty careful that in practice you aren't breaking the law, even unintentionally. Other countries don't have these standards, or if they do, they aren't enforced as they are in the States."

"Mandela was also concerned about how to stop Brain Drain, how does one retain the technical knowledge and subsequent advancement in one's country? In the long run this was huge, because the people with the know how must remain to keep the place strong economically. Mandela would have to wrestle with this issue, since historically the technical skills had only been installed in the White population. How did he keep the Whites engaged and supportive during this transition of power and growth? If he didn't, his beloved country could be set back for generations, if all the know-how left in a fear-filled migratory shift."

"Later, while Mandela was President, he was successful at building a cloak of cohesion to wrap around all of his fellow countrymen. But after he retired and became quite an older man, that wasn't true with his successor. The Brain Drain began, and one could argue that South Africa has been in decline ever since. A whole lot of competent capable South Africans have since left to go to places like Australia, New Zealand, England and the United States. The Wilkinson's' own children were an example of this. Their daughter went to High School in South Africa, but then she left for Australia to attend college and medical school. After graduation, she remained, married an Aussie and to this day resides and practices medicine in her new country."

"Their oldest son, also went to college in Australia. He married an Australian and lives in Adelaide with his wife and children. They are entrepreneurial farmers. Which leaves their youngest child as the only remaining South African resident. After attending college in South Africa, he works as a commercial pilot for a local airline. He now has one child with his South African wife. This one in three retention ratio is probably pretty typical of the national statistics, and it is that kind of brain drain, that can hurt any country long term."

I understood the delicacy of this plight, when I contrasted my living experiences in Philadelphia and Atlanta. The former had suffered from chronic, formidable brain drain. For example, many smart students came from around the world to the University of Pennsylvania. For years, residents in local neighborhoods surrounding the Ivy League school followed the sirens' call to the safer status of the suburbs, after being slowly worn down by both petty and violent crimes. Many brilliant people came and received elite educations at Penn's medical, dental and business schools.

These same future professionals, would rent out the locals' old homes since they were now non-saleable due to fear. Upon graduation, the students fled my city in terror back to their homes, spreading tales of pillage across the world. Over the years, on different continents, I heard many riffs on this repetitive tale. Car windows smashed so often it was better just to not have one, having to keep a few dollars in a pocket to pay off the homeless guy on the corner or suffer the thinly veiled threat of assault.

More often than not I heard Penn graduates say, "I hated Philadelphia. I got a great education while there, but I couldn't wait to get the hell out of there when I was done!" As a proud native, this always made me very sad. As a frustrated brand ambassador for the City of Brotherly Love, I thought these neighborhoods should have been the prime focus for concerted efforts at crime reduction. Because whether the city recognized it or not, the University of Pennsylvania was really its global curb appeal or its postcard mailed to the rest of the world.

In my personal urban history, Mayor Rendell had accomplished this very thing, over in the center city district. He created a battalion of uniformed street cleaners, who occasionally turned into accidental crime fighters. They were part of the pivotal pioneers that brought the millennials into the city to live again. But this change hadn't crossed over the Schuylkill River into Ivy country.

This was what Mandela faced on a larger scale, how to coalesce and keep all of his country's citizens engaged and on their new path? He recognized that human ingenuity and creativity were the magic key. He was wise in knowing that it would be a much longer walk to freedom for his country, if they didn't figure out how to retain and grow the knowledge base.

I pictured Mandela sitting in his cell for twenty-six years, combing through variables on future outcomes, determining optimal methods to coax people to coalesce. I thought of the author, Mark Booth's quote, "It isn't generals and presidents that have changed the world. It is one person sitting alone in one room with one brain, that changes the world." Such a fitting description for Mandela's life. The skeptic that I am, Keith's conversation with Mandela brought me hope. There was at least one world leader far seeing enough to give a sh*t here in the present. But how long would it last, as Mandela was in the twilight of his life?

The hairs on my neck stood up like tiny antennae. Perhaps it was my sixth sense. Maybe my body knew before I knew, that one day, Keith, would take me to the very place where Mandela had stayed. We would walk the very halls together where Madiba wrote and documented *His Long Walk to Freedom*, upon his release from Robben Island.

My thoughts turned to my new home in Atlanta. My experience in Atlanta was the opposite of Brain Drain. It was a magnet for young up and comers, the city was growing, the professionals were flocking to this land of opportunity, including myself. I had been

so excited about my own race to independence in
Atlanta.  But after this night of intellect-stretching
adventure, a corner of my heart was tugging to stay
right here, where it knew it had come home.


*~ Each Destiny requires a long walk to Freedom.*
*What is Yours? ~*

# IF YOU ARE WAITING ON ME YOU ARE BACKING UP

*~ Reduce anxiety, Say what you Mean ~*

By this time, we had pretty much closed down the bar. We had nicknamed one dapper, mature man with happy feet, The Dancer. As the only solo man in the bar, he had his pick of numerous women hungry for a dance partner. As we traveled the Blue Train in our minds with Mandela, the Dancer was flinging, twirling, twisting and shouting. But the music had come to an end. As the evening wound down, the young, efficient bartender, shared her own personal miracle. She had a hundred percent recovery from Stage IV breast cancer. She woke up ever day happy to be healthy and alive. It was the first of many heartfelt conversations with bartenders across the globe.

I asked Keith for a South African story that illustrated his value building principle: Get More of the Good Stuff.

He thought for a moment and volunteered, "The UG2 Reef." At that moment an ever-ready valet appeared at Keith's elbow with the keys to his car and a happy go lucky grin on his face.

Startled, Keith asked, "Are we it? Did we close the joint down?" With that he reached in his pocket and said "Hold on young man, you don't work for free, do you?"

If it was possible the young man's smile stretched even further, as he thanked Keith for the tip. The college kid looked as chipper as if it was one in the afternoon instead of one in the morning. Oh, to have that kind of youthful energy again! Then I realized it must be contagious or in the air down here. I had been up since five for the early flight. Carpe Diem for sure. This was the most spellbinding conversation I had had in my life, on numerous levels. I was unsure if it would ever repeat itself, because Keith had surely stopped my clock.

As Keith walked me back to his car, the Southern gentleman that he was, he asked, "Well, I don't know about you, but this evening was not what I expected." As he opened the passenger door for me, I settled into the bucket seat, and realized I had not felt this relaxed in a long time.

As Keith clambered into the driver's side, I murmured, "You can say that again."

In his distinctive sonorous tones that my ears couldn't get enough of, Keith continued, "I've spent my career picking people. Hands down, I would pick you every time. You are the most interesting woman

I've met in a very long time. Erica, you have all the votes."

Shocked by Keith's forthright, blunt-edged honesty, I was speechless, which is saying something in itself. Keith's "all the votes" comment was a board room reference. When a CEO at a publicly traded corporation is pitching a business plan to his board of outside directors, he or she needs them to vote on it before proceeding. When Keith made board pitches, he would use this stock phrase of his to clearly tell the board that he was all in on a particular idea, and he was just waiting on them to work it through and hopefully approve.

Suddenly feeling a bit nervous and not in control at all, I stammered, "What do you mean?"

"Erica, I don't know how to say this anymore clearly, but if you are waiting on me you are backing up."

With my ears ringing from all the blood rushing to my head (as Coldplay sang), I'm not even sure if I was capable of responding at that point. I saw images of my little daughters and my late hours spent in solitude at my desk. I could hear Keith talking about how his mother Sarah Belle would never allow him to drop me off in a parking lot in the dead of night to drive myself home. He would take me to my hotel, then I could pick up my car in the morning, which I found so endearing.

There was an ache in my heart as we arrived in front of my hotel's lobby. It was as if a magnet was pulling us toward each other. Our faces were inches apart as we looked into each other's eyes. Much being said with no words passing our lips.

"Thank you for a wonderful evening. I loved it," was about all I could muster. As I stumbled out into the darkness with tears welling up in my eyes.

The next morning, I was up super early, and took a taxi to retrieve my car. I stopped at City Place, a lovely little outdoor mall completed by palm trees, to pick up some souvenirs for the girls, when Keith called my Blackberry. He wanted to make sure that I was successful in finding my car. The ache was pretty palpable. Even though we spoke only in small pleasantries, there was an underlying raging river of emotions. Trying to think of an excuse to contact Keith soon, I mumbled something about his Florida Intangible Tax Return that was due by the end of the month, and we disconnected. Belatedly, I then wistfully realized, I did not get to hear the story about the UG2 reef, and probably never would.

*~ Recognize when Lightning is in the Bottle,*
*for it Doesn't happen often ~*

# ON MY OWN AGAIN

*~ Pursue lifelong learning Achievements,*
*they will always be Part of You ~*

The summer was flying by in Hot-lanta. I literally
drove around Atlanta in inexplicable circular highways
as I got to know my new client base of Delta
executives. Alas, I was required to fly up to Philly, to
wrap up my last two final exams, to complete my
Masters in Taxation at Villanova University's School of
Law.

Upon reflection, I am not really sure how I
remained standing that calendar year. Years later,
Keith nicknamed me shoehorn, and I hate to admit he
was right. In the previous year, I had accepted a
transfer to Atlanta, ramped up career requirements to
make partner, moved solo across states with my two
daughters, bought a house, enrolled them in a new
school, and co-created a corporate executive financial
planning program for Delta Airline's executives.
Somehow, I hadn't gotten fired or had a stroke. About
ten years before, while working, I had studied and
passed the CPA exam, then the CFP's planner exam.
Now, I had two remaining courses to finish my

Masters in Taxation, but this unattainable Holy Grail was back in Philly, and I was exhausted.

*~ Always invest in Yourself,*
*You are your best Return on Investment ~*

# TAX DEFERRALS

## ~ *Make Better what You already Have* ~

It was at this point, that I called Keith, while planning my home town visit. I had some tax planning advice for him. He had a SEP-IRA, otherwise known as a Simplified Employee Pension-Individual Retirement Account. We were firming up his final annual contribution limit.

If you are an entrepreneur, you have self-employment income and you too should consider owning a SEP to maximize retirement savings and reduce current income taxes. Keith served on a number of company's boards, and what he earned in board fees was self-employment income too.

Taxpayers don't necessarily believe that one can still contribute income into an IRA, after retirement. This would be a fallacy, for you can, if you receive a 1099-MISC or have self-employment income from a business. Take advantage of this IRA on steroids! Instead of $6,000 you can save up to $56,000 annually with a SEP. Once running, you aren't required to contribute to it every year, so it is great if you have big swings of income between years. (This does not work for royalties or lottery winnings, because you didn't actively earn it.) It's one of the most inexpensive ways to save the most for retirement as a solo self-employed person with no employees.

As we wrapped up this part of our conversation, we were joking about which one of Keith's value principles did a SEP fit into. Was this reducing the cost of capital, as it reduced tax? Or was it making better what you already had, meaning one's life?

I mentioned my dreaded trip to Philadelphia for my two finals. With a touch of surprise, Keith said, "Why I'm up here myself already! I am down the Jersey Shore with my children." With some calendar comparisons, we realized we could meet up for a lunch, before I flew back to Atlanta, which we planned. I confessed how stressed and ill prepared I felt for this last push at the Master's in Taxation. Keith gave me encouragement to finish strong. Once I had the degree completed, no one could ever take that designation away, it would always be part of me. I knew he was right.

*~ Take care of Yourself, so you can Care for Others ~*

# THE UG2 REEF

## ~ *Get more of the Good Stuff* ~

Before we hung up, I reminded Keith of where we had left off that first night. I hoped when we met again, that he wouldn't mind telling me about the UG2 Reef in South Africa.

"Well there is no time like the present, if you have time now, and this story definitely fits into my Value Principle of go get more of the good stuff," Keith responded. It was easy to banish billable hours and plane reservations from my mind, as Keith picked up the beginning threads of the story. Little did I know then how many business stories we would share in the future that would fit into these four categories.

"So, you may remember, the deal we cut with Terence was a complex deal, so it actually covered ahh bunch of my Increase Value principles. But definitely More of the Good Stuff applied to the UG2 Reef. In my view, this can include a bunch-a things such as Invent Something. And that is what we had done at Engelhard when we built the catalytic converter that created the new demand. And Lonrho definitely got more of the good stuff by figuring out how to mine the UG2 Reef."

Even though I knew this was an ore mining story, I was still picturing coral reefs under the ocean. At this point one of my peers, who definitely won the class clown awards throughout his life, smashed his distorted face up against my office's glass window, and tried to get me to crack up. It was like an interment camp sometimes, levity helped break up the grind. But today, I was not going to be deterred in my own fact-finding mining expedition, so I just crossed my eyes and stuck out my tongue, unfazed by these adolescent antics.

Inwardly, I smiled knowing that no one I worked with would understand at all, what was going on here between Keith and me. In the office, there were always jokes about wealthy clients re-marrying a younger woman and all the negative comments would begin, the trophy wife and gold digger jibes. Then the bad tax jokes such as "He better have an air tight pre-nup! This ain't gonna last!"

But there was a level of fear here too, because this relationship could cause me grave career risk, the def-con nuclear option kind. In the wrong place and time, it could cost me my job. We had all kinds of ethical rules about who we could fraternize with and still be viewed as independent. Thank God there were a few states separating me from my fast-becoming favorite client, we were going to need some physical borders.

"A Reef is the term applied to the ore body and how it is distinguished as a separate entity from the earth that surrounds it. Platinum ore bodies are all generally formed on the same relative two to three percent slope inclining down into the earth. They can go on for kilometers. There are two dimensions to the reef. There is the width of the strike, the width of the ore body itself and the incline that the strike goes into the earth. In the case of the Merensky Reef, it was almost thirty kilometers wide. The UG2 was a little bit shorter, somewhere around twenty. The ore body itself was about one meter or four feet wide. So, you were mining, if you will, the ham out of the middle of a ham sandwich. The real technology was keeping the mine from collapsing and getting the ore from below ground to above ground without anybody getting killed so it could be processed. The ore body will outcrop at some point, then the trail will run on an angle deep into the earth for miles, or kilometers if you are South African. One ton of ore in the Merensky Reef would translate to about twelve grams of platinum group metals and in that reef about eight of those twelve grams were platinum. The remaining four grams were divided into palladium, rhodium, ruthenium iridium and osmium, what are called the platinum group metals. The Merensky Reef had almost no chromium in there but the deeper UG2 Reef had all kinds ahh chromium mixed in."

As Keith warmed to his subject his latent Southern softened consonants started to appear in his speech patterns. I found it fascinating, listening to this broad, brawny man talking about complex technical topics with a soft drawl.

"The original strike was the Merensky Reef. All the mining companies knew how to mine that one. Those scientific formulas were mastered to separate out the platinum and the related metals found in the same ore body. All the mining rights were established, everyone knew what was what. But also, everyone in the industry knew there was this second reef recently discovered called the UG2. It was directly below the Merensky Reef, so first off it was more difficult to get to. But after boring down to it, people realized that the composition of the metals was a lot messier than the Merensky. People would have to discover new formulas to cost effectively separate the metal from the trash."

"This is where my friend Terence at Lonrho, had something that the big guys did not. Their technical guy, Ian Hossey, had figured out the science to refine the UG2 Reef. They were it, no one else knew how to do it. Therefore, there was no competition to mine that reef. If you drilled down deeper to access the ore body, most people couldn't refine it to the .9999 purity required for industrial use. Their competitors didn't know it yet. But Lonrho had beaten them all to the punch. They took the road less traveled and figured out the new formulas, so they could get More of the Good Stuff."

"Once the competitors knew what Lonrho had discovered, they tried to buy Ian. But he wasn't going to leave Terence, they had a blood brother handshake. He was very honorable and they had taken these big risks together. Then some competitors tried to steal his formulas. Ian's office was ransacked looking for his work! But he kept his fresh ideas in a safe location elsewhere. Ian didn't tell anyone except Terence where that was. In case he was killed, Terence would be able to continue the work."

With that three staff people were lined up at my door with tax returns to be reviewed. We confirmed our upcoming lunch in Wilmington, Delaware, which was close to the Philadelphia airport for my return flight to my new Atlanta home. I signed off with a half-joking clip, "I think I will stick to taxes, I don't think anyone's going to kill me for a secret formula." But I could picture a career fratricide.

*~ Take the time to Tinker
and develop Your own Formulas ~*

# THE LITTLE I

### ~ *Take the Road less Traveled and Enjoy the Journey* ~

After finishing my last exam for my Master's, I drove South on the Blue Route. Instead of turning North on I-95 to head directly to the airport, I drove South towards Wilmington, Delaware. It so happened that Keith was wrapping up a board meeting for a bank, and was going to return to the Jersey shore, where he kept a beach house. Keith was staying at the Hotel Du Pont, where we met in the lobby for lunch. It had that Art Deco 1930's feel, with the original polished brass around doorways and dark paneling sprinkled along the walls.

One of the cool things about this small city, is that all big wheeler dealers are packed into this tiny geographically restrained "fish bowl". If you've ever seen the Koi in a pond all piled up on top of each other, or the Florida Manatees packing into the warmer waters at utility plants, you will have a visual image of what I mean. In big sprawling metropolises like Los Angeles, Dallas or even New York City there are a lot of quiet corners to go make a deal. Not in

Wilmington everyone knows who is talking with whom.

It had been a number of months since I'd last seen Keith's face and his intelligent eyes. It was like a crushing blow to the solar plexus all over again. He knocked me breathless and his powerful voice literally made my ears ring. I had wondered if it was an aberrant reaction last time, but it clearly was not. My cool, calm collected self just hit a brick wall.

"Let's walk over to the Wilmington Club where we can have the best fast food in America, for lunch!"

I came to a screeching halt, "Whaaaaat!" In this chummy little town, EVERY executive belonged to this club and they ate lunch together on a regular basis. At this point in time, it was definitely a men's only membership, and pretty much only men ate in these refined hallowed halls. Women weren't normally invited as guests at this point in time. This seemingly innocent invitation to lunch confirmed my previous naming convention: Braveheart.

In Keith's swashbuckling style, he crowed, answering my unspoken question of not belonging, "Hell no one will care." I'm usually pretty nonchalant about this kind of stuff, but I was definitely rattled over this unplanned escapade. When I worked for the institution, I dressed my best, and psychologically prepared myself before walking into places of power. Today, I felt like I was walking into the Lion's Den, the only saving grace was that I would be on Keith's arm instead of alone.

When we first arrived, we were met by the club manager, Mr. Marcus Mayr, who had presided over the club in a seemingly effortless forty years of service, as only European Club managers can do. I don't blush easily, but I could feel the heat creeping up my neck. Feeling like the uncouth American in this formal setting, I shook the suave Mr. Mayr's hand as he treated me like the crown princess of Sweden.

At the time, I did not know what a great friend Marcus was with Keith. They had spent years together and knew each other well. Marcus knew what he was up to. Keith hadn't been personally happy in a long time.

As I was hiding behind the cut crystal glassware, Keith hailed someone over to make introductions. Quickly, I tried to pick the dried skin off of my chapped lips, behind the beautifully starched napkin. With a flourish, Keith announced, "Erica I want to introduce you to Ed Woolard, the former Chairman and CEO of DuPont. I like to remind Ed that DuPont was 'the little French paint company down the street from Hercules'." With that they both had a chuckle, since DuPont was significantly larger than Hercules. This jab was quintessential Keith, the part of him that I loved, this Take No Prisoners attitude.

That conversation was interesting, because Ed shared some details of his recent experiences firing and then re-hiring Steve Jobs, while he served on the board of Apple. Years later, we read Steve's own verification in Walter Isaacson's penned biography on Jobs. In essence, Steve Jobs insisted on referring to himself as the interim CEO, lest he forget he was fired from his own company by his own board. He expected and planned for the ideas and the institution to far outlast his leadership. Keith often says, "The cool winds blew through my office as soon as I announced by retirement six months out. Don't be surprised, because no one cares what you think anymore, they are going down the hall to the next guy's office."

The temporary status of a CEO was effectively branded by Steve Jobs as the iCEO. Of course, this transitory concept was embraced and extended by Jobs in his products: the iPhone, iPod, iPad, each product only an interim step leading the consumer down the profitable path of required renewal.

Keith referenced Walt Mahler, one of his great mentors. "There are two kinds of managers. One is an institutional leader and the other is a sh*t disturber. One leaves an institution and the second one leaves a pile of disturbed sh*t. And Ahh swear that I've never met a manager that didn't fit into one kind or the other. Now I know this is one of Walt's proverbs, but I've claimed it as my own!"

I couldn't help myself, "Well, I know Steve Jobs has changed the world but after watching a few TV movies about his management style, I would say he also left a few piles of disturbed sh*t! So maybe he was a hybrid."


~ *Watch how others Lead,*
*and Decide what to Apply* ~

# HIGH FIDELITY
# AND THE POISON PILL

## ~ *Follow Your own Instincts* ~

Clearly, long discussions over a shared table was going to be the crux of my relationship with this man, because we picked up right where we left off. As the club manager and his team busied themselves around the club, we continued to talk over coffee.

"I think it was about 1996, and I hadn't been CEO that long. By that point, I had been President of Operations for about two years. One day we looked up and we noticed that someone was buying our stock. The buying volume was up about two hundred thousand shares per day for about two months straight, above our historical average. So, we were pretty sure someone was accumulating our stock, we just didn't really know who it was. To try and find out who the buyer was, we hired a New York firm, some firm like Pershing. But I'm not sure if that is right. They got a little bit of the lead that a lot of the trades were coming from the Boston area, and then were being fed into New York. So, we started looking at companies in that area that had that level of buying ability. Certainly, Fidelity was one of the contenders, but we never really tied it down."

"Every ninety days, companies have to file a thing called a 13D, if they own more than five percent of a company's stock. Well, at least that's what it was back in those days. So, the 13D did indeed show that Fidelity was the buyer, and they had finished at nine percent of Hercules' shares. They owned us in a single mutual fund a value fund. That would make sense at the time, because we were indeed a company that had increased in value. They had missed the first big run up in stock price, and they were trying to see if there was any juice left in the lemon. Based on this buy, they had concluded in fact that there was some profit left to squeeze out."

"They hadn't identified themselves to us, they had quietly bought us anonymously. They did not approach us, the management to request any one on one meetings. As we looked back at some of the people that attended our industrial conferences, Fidelity was definitely in our Hercules afternoon break-out sessions after the big morning show. There would be about thirteen or fourteen big chemical companies participating in the chemical conference."

"A few weeks after the 13d came out, Jim Rapp, our investor relations guy got a phone call from one of Fidelity's young analysts for one of their big Value Funds. He asked if he could coordinate a meeting with our company's management. Jim came to see me and confirmed what we sort of suspected. "

"Fidelity had made sure to stay below a ten percent ownership threshold, so they didn't trigger our shareholder rights' plan, otherwise known as a poison pill. It is a technique whereby the poison pill refers to a trigger that significantly dilutes all existing shareholders to the point where the potential acquirer no longer has a viable investment, when they 'swallow the pill' by buying too many shares."

"Jim asked me if I wanted them to come to us in Delaware, or go see them in Boston. I said, 'Hell no, they own close to ten percent of the company, we will go there.' We made a date for a week or so later to go to Boston and meet with them in the middle of the day. We had the company airplane so we could meet that morning and fly right into Boston. We then took a car to their headquarters."

"A very young male analyst introduced himself and took us to the meeting. He opened the door into an amphitheater, there was a table and three chairs on our side, and one chair on his side. There was spacious seating on each level, holding about thirty-five people. The young man introduced the group as his colleagues, but he didn't identify each one of them. They ranged in gender and age, but there was clearly one guy that stood out to me from the beginning as the elderly statesman or 'Mr. Gray Hair'."

"I introduced the people with me, our CFO and
our Vice President of Investor Relations.  I started,
'We are here to talk to you about the investment you
made in our company.  We are really happy that you've
done that and we think we will be a good investment
for you.  We are a fairly unique company.  Since we are
not a straightforward, business, I think we need to
explain our complexities to you.  To set the stage, I
need only five minutes to explain our company's long-
term strategy so you understand who we are and what
we are going to be.  We have seven entirely different
businesses, all with very different customer profiles
requiring different chemistry research work.
Therefore, our work requires different kinds of plants
located around the world'."

"Why did it require being all around the world?
Was it international tax opportunities?" I asked, always
thinking like a tax person.

Keith replied, "No not really, that was always a
plus if a tax strategy helped optimize an operation
decision after the fact. But the decision to build a plant
was big money.  If you didn't get it right you could
cause big problems.  And the scary part, was you
wouldn't always know until four or five years into the
future after the plant was up and operating.  Our main
reason to build a plant in another country was to be as
close as possible to the raw materials.  For example, at
Hercules we had paper making plants on the tops of
Norway, Finland and Sweden, so we could make paper

right at the forests. Paper would cost ten dollars a page, if we brought the trees back to America and made paper back home. We would all be wiping our a$$es with papyrus right now at that rate."

Keith picked up the Fidelity story again. After our segue into Scandinavia, I reoriented myself back into the Bostonian Fidelity lecture hall. He continued:

"I named the seven different businesses that we nicknamed franchises, because each was really unique. We had paper chemicals, water treatment, resins, cellulosic-based polymer producers, each with very, very different uses. We had just sold our aerospace business to Alliant, which was a big piece of our last period's earnings, so Fidelity had missed some of that increase in the stock price. But they were still hoping to squeeze some of the juice out of our lemon."

"I continued to address the group, 'I'm going to take another minute on each business and give you each operational strategy. Then I will give you our overall financial strategy and how we will always be an investment grade debt. We manage our debt to equity ratio very carefully, and we are very sensitive to tax rates'."

"That was about as far as I got when the young guy interrupted, 'That is really all very interesting but we really want to know what you are going to be doing in earnings in the next year.' I continued, 'I only asked for five minutes to give you broader perspective, we have a longer-term view than next year.' I started up again and didn't get further than a minute when the same young buck demanded, 'Mr. Elliott, we really need to know your thinking in the next two to three quarters'."

"This is in essence the financial concept of giving guidance, which I-ahhh hate! I turned and looked at our two guys and I said 'It is time to close up and head out of here, thanks for the invitation'. I think the kid musta been trying to make an impression with his bosses. After my announcement, the kid turned purple and he got really aggressive and loud like investment bankers always do. 'Where do you think you are going? We own ten percent of your company! You are refusing to talk to us'!"

"As I slammed my briefcase shut, I responded, 'Before we came here, we did some research on YOU, and the fund that bought our shares. What we found out was that your average holding time of your fund's investment shares are only between three and six months, before you dump it. I told you that this is a long term buy for you. So, if your average holding time is only three to six months, why should I give a f*ck what you think?"

At this juncture, I about fell out of my chair laughing. Then I recalled I was in a refined eating establishment, and ended up choking on a fit of stifled giggles. I wish I had ten percent of the courage my

Braveheart had! Did I just say MY Braveheart? Keith continued:

"We turned towards the double doors and started to walk out. Suddenly, the old guy in the room jumped up from the back row and made his way down to the floor. Slight flushed Mr. Gray Hair said, 'Wait! I am the Chief Investment Officer of the fund! We want to understand your company better, so please sit back down and talk to us'."

"So, we started by spending about a half hour talking about our complexities and therefore the unpredictable nature of our outcomes in the short term. By then, Mr. Gray Hair sat stock still in his chair, with his knees crossed, thoughtfully rubbing his chin. 'Wow it's a really complicated business.' I agreed with him and continued to give him examples."

"From the outside looking in it would be difficult for you to understand how complex we are relative to the size of our company. For example, we have the resins division where we have two plants. One is in South Georgia and the other in the United Kingdom. The company's first business was black powder, which ya know makes dynamite. When the U.S. Justice Department spun off Hercules from DuPont in 1912, it was part of the big anti-trust regulations."

"Oh, yah mean Teddy Roosevelt the Trust Buster?" I chimed in.

Keith nodded his head and continued to recount his Fidelity détente story:

"Farmers in Georgia would use the black powder and dynamite to blast the stumps out of the ground so they could turn the land into farmland. So, the early Hercules guys would buy these monster stumps take them to our labs. Then they would press out the rosin from the pine stump. The scientists began to mix it with a few other things, and it had a lot of practical uses. We put it in paper making machines. The rosin was like magic it made wet strength, which makes think like the paper towel work. It also made sizing which keeps ink from running off the page, the stickiness in effect. We also sold the sticky raw resin to adhesive companies like 3M and Loctite for use in adhesives."

"Later our research team discovered you could also make adhesives out of hydrocarbons and that was the other plant we had in Europe. Hydrocarbons are the key elements in petroleum and natural gas. The end adhesive product was similar to the rosin based one, but the raw materials were obviously completely different from tree stumps. And the processes were completely different, since these were custom mixtures dependent on customers' orders. For example, our chemical end product for the adhesive on sticky notes was completely different from the one that went into school glue. The process for hydrocarbon-based resins was a mixture of oil based with a similar resin molecule. Since it was so much thicker, you had to add water and other fluids to thin it out."

Keith continued, "So we ended up having this great conversation with Mr. Gray Hair, who brought his chair down to sit with us. Also, he allowed some of the people in the back of the room to ask questions and we ended up being there for about three or four hours. It ended up being a really great meeting. Because we took the time to talk to each other, they ended up holding the stock for three and half to four years. When they finally decided to sell it, the CIO called me personally. He notified us that we made an adequate return, but it was time for them to start selling. He assured me he wasn't going to dump it so it wouldn't have a shock effect on the share price."

*~ Do your own Research, and be Prepared
to Walk Away from the Table ~*

# DO YOUR OWN ANALYSIS

*~ There is a time to Share Only*
*what is Required ~*

As the never ending encyclopedia of information, Keith continued:

"These were the times when companies started providing serious quarter to quarter guidance to Wall Street's financial analysts. I just refused to do it, my predecessor wanted to do it, and he did give guidance in his last few years as CEO. But once I got the job I refused."

"When I attended my first big chemical conference as CEO, it was sponsored by somebody like Morgan or Goldman. But anyway, I announced, 'I'm going to go from providing quarterly guidance to annual guidance because we are a complicated company with a lot of moving parts, a whole lotta different customer bases, serving a whole lotta different industries. Many of our customers were cyclical that we served. They went up and down with various economies in the world. Since we are affected by currencies around the world, it's nigh on impossible for us to predict every quarter. So, I think I am actually doing a disservice to the investors if I give guidance. It is crazy to me that if you miss your earnings by a penny a share that your stock price goes down ten percent, or if you beat it by two pennies a share it goes up ten percent. I think it really is madness.' Which of course mah statement made a lotta analysts pissed off, to say the least."

"Often I would say, 'Most of you went to the best business schools in the world, for God's sake you can go figure it out. God forbid you actually have to do your job and analyze something. Why do we have to do your work for you?' But to be fair, I did this kind of conversation only in one on one phone calls with analysts."

"To this day I still hate that companies get pressured into giving guidance. I'm a member of the board of several NYSE companies. In my view, it is clear that providing short term Earnings Per Share guidance forces CEOs to think short term rather than doing what is right for the business. I-ahhh believe that this practice continues to have a negative impact on publicly owned companies, especially manufacturing companies making them less competitive and relevant in the world today. The damn analysts from their fancy schools and ridiculously high salaries, should earn it rather than intimidating management into doing their work for them!"

By now Keith was definitely fired up. I decided to use some levity to defuse a bit of the tension build-up.

"Talking to financial analysts sounds a lot like when I have to talk to the IRS! I tell taxpayers, that is why they need me to advocate upon their behalf. Often, they tell the IRS things that are not required that can open up a whole other can of worms for them. But to your point, I believe stockholders must share some responsibility, which is all of us with an IRA or 401(k). And the lawyers had to have their share of the blame because it was case law like the Revlon case that got us all down this road of worshipping at the shareholders' feet instead of protecting the institution that actually employed everybody."

By this time, Keith had recovered some calmness, and finished up, "However, I do think that providing strategic guidance regarding long term issues such as growth rates, expected tax rates, long term capital spending, and expected long term cash flow and liquidity expectations is important planning information for investors."

~ *Be Brave enough to Fight for what is Ethical* ~

# YOU HAVE ALL THE VOTES

## ~ *Practice Speaking your Mind* ~

By this time, we were the last to leave the Wilmington Club, a future signpost of many meals to come. It was definitely time for me to head North to the Philadelphia Airport, so I could make my plane home to Hannah and Chloe. We walked back to the Hotel Du Pont to have our cars brought around to go our separate ways.

In that reverberant baritone, Keith picked up a javelin he had launched at our first departure. "Erica, I told you this when we met for dinner in Florida. You are the most fascinating woman I've met in a long time. I would love to spend more time with you. Obviously, our lives are complicated. You have two small children and a career. Therefore, you have all the votes."

Again, I was struck speechless. My heart and stomach were pulsating yes and yes. My head was screaming a resounding, "No, Erica! What you are you nuts? Do you really think this cosmopolitan man and erudite executive has anything in common with you? What if we went down this road and Keith comes to his senses, and calls this fanciful escapade

213

off? What if by that time, my firm has figured out I'm seeing a client, and they fire me? What if they fire me and Keith dumps me at the same time?"

Then I thought of all the gossipy knowing nudges and whispers about Erica and her sugar daddy. Then I pictured the church people calling to tell me God had spoken to them about what my life's requirements were and they certainly didn't include Keith.

Suddenly, I was angry, I was tired of living my life for other people and their judgmental expectations, that really shouldn't matter at the end of the day. But the thought of risking my career for a fascinating man that would probably tire of me was still quite terrifying.

All I could muster was a "Are you sure? "

With a broad Cheshire grin, Keith replied, "My Momma didn't raise no fool!"

With that my car appeared first, and Keith followed me over to open my driver's side door in front of the lobby where people were bustling about. From under Keith's lowered eyelids, I could see the kindness in his hazel irises. The minister of my interior was walking through the rooms of my mind again, turning over each object of my terror and examining each one. It was soothing, that he could see me as I was, terrified. He leaned forward and gently kissed me on the mouth.

He murmured again, "You are an amazing woman, take all the time you need to think about it."

Hands still shaking, I drove through the charging rain onto I-95's entrance ramp. With the heater blasting, I fumbled for my phone charger. My mind was whirling through an endless list of possible outcomes. But, Keith's gifts of time and choice, were so freeing and valued. Somewhere down in the pit of my stomach, all felt right with the world. A small candle of trust was lit for the first time in a long while, as I felt again Keith's lips firmly claiming mine.

*~ Gently listen, build trust and you can create a lifetime partnership. ~*

༜

# ACKNOWLEDGEMENTS

Hannah and Chloe, how I love you both.  Kahlil Gibran's poetic words express it so much better than I ever could.  You are both "the living arrows sent forth from my bow... you have come through me, not to me... for your souls' dwell in the house of tomorrow." I can't wait to see where your life journeys take you both.

As I sit here in 2019, writing these words, times have clearly changed from the days of telexes, faxes, landlines, Blackberries and CD changers.  As I write this, I am listening to "Cinema", a song that our daughters shared with me.   Benny Benassi's dance hit is reminiscent of my Latin Freestyle favorites from the eighties.  Those lyrics could have been commissioned by me for my Sweet Keith:

*"I could watch ya for a lifetime.  You're my favorite movie.  You are a cinema.  Forever fascinating.  Action.  Thriller.  I could watch ya forever.  Love you just the way you are."*

These lyrics are the musical score for my personal movie, playing in my head.  Keith, Hannah and Chloe: I love you all and I can't wait to see what movie plays next.

∽∾

# RECOMMENDED READING LIST

*Mahlerisms* ~ by Walter R. Mahler

*How Effective Executives Interview* ~ by Walter R. Mahler

*Long Walk to Freedom* ~ by Nelson Mandela

*Wisdom for a young CEO* ~ by Douglas Barry

*Africa: The Biography of a Continent* ~ by John Reader

༄༅

# WORK WITH ME

I am the proud co-founder of BizBooks.Expert LLC, where we offer boutique tax and accounting services to select clients. I have a soft spot for all courageous entrepreneurs out there and am thrilled to help them spread their wings into the world of independent prosperity and success.

There are many ways that you can work with me, beginning with an introductory entrepreneurial program, ongoing intensive support and individual business development management.

For start-ups and small ventures, I co-created Endeavor University, an educational subscription program of video tutorials to get you going quickly on a prudent budget, with immediate access. Find it at **www.endeavoruniversity.thinkific.com**

As my reader, you are always privy to special invitations and selected workshops. To stay informed, you can visit our business' page at **www.bizbooks.expert** and sign up for our newsletter.

For all other inquiries about my various books and artistic endeavors, you can always reach out to me at **www.ericaswensonelliott.com**.

## ABOUT THE AUTHOR

Erica Elliott has an unusual set of gifts. As a prominent tax accountant and also an author and artist at heart, she finds great joy in creating order from chaos and inspiration through her writing. Where other people get dizzy with numbers, she sees clarity and creates profitable, practical magic. The author was brought up in a quite unorthodox yet loving household: friendly with Healers and finding purpose through communal connection. This upbringing allowed her to see people, circumstances and things in unusual ways. Her early memories were first falling in love with numbers, words, and then drawing, all symbols pointing us along the mystical journey of life. She encourages everyone to follow and recognize all of their unique, diverse gifts, no matter how many they carry. Yes, you can be an accountant, artist and author!

Visit the author online at **ericaswensonelliott.com.**

Made in the USA
Coppell, TX
06 March 2021